AN ENGLISHMAN IN NEW YORK

The Memoirs of John Miskin Prior 1948-49

For Elloise and Candice, whose Grandfather loved them very much indeed.

Copyright

An Englishman in New York:
The memoirs of John Miskin Prior 1948-49
ISBN 9780645118742
10 9 8 7 6 5 4 3

Copyright © 2020 by Simon Michael Prior

All rights reserved. No part of this book may be reproduced or transmitted in any form or by any means without written permission from the author.

An Englishman in New York: The Memoirs of John Miskin Prior 1948-49

Contents

INTRODUCTION 5
1. HURRICANE IN THE ATLANTIC..................................7
2. AN UNWELCOME CUSTOMS INSPECTION 12
3. DAZZLING NEON AND UNBELIEVABLE SKYSCRAPERS............14
4. A LUCKY BREAK 18
5. NEWS OF AN EXCITING TRIP 22
6. WONDERFUL SOCIAL INVITATIONS..........................24
7. AN EXCITING TOUR OF NEW YORK STATE 27
8. A PRESENTATION FROM EISENHOWER 31
9. AMERICAN FOOTBALL..38
10. AMERICANS HAVE NO CONCEPT OF THE WAR 41
11. A WEALTHY CONNECTICUT FAMILY......................44
12. THE BEST INTERVIEWEE ON ABC TV 48
13. THE DANCE OF THE SEVEN VEILS 50
14. YOU MAY NOT HAVE A GIRL IN YOUR ROOM 53
15. GIVE 'EM HELL...57
16. THE TRUMAN MIRACLE..62
17. A FOREIGN AFFAIR 68
18. A FUTURE KING 70
19. IT'S LIKE EATING FIRE 74
20. A BOSTON TEA PARTY 77
21. TOO MANY CAKES AND BEER...............................81
22. DELIGHTFUL VASSAR COLLEGE GIRLS 84
23. CHORUS GIRLS DRESSED UP AS POODLES 89
24. POUGHKEEPSIE CHRISTMAS 93

25. COCKTAILS WITH THE ROOSEVELTS 95
26. A PRIVATE CHAT WITH ELLIOT ROOSEVELT 103
27. THE FOOLISHNESS OF MAN AND THE WISDOM OF GOD .. 107
28. A RICH WALL STREET LAWYER 110
29. GONE WITH THE WIND 114
30. IS SIXTY PARTICULARLY OLD? 118
31. PETITPAS 122
32. CANADIAN RADIO 125
33. MARDI GRAS 129
34. SLAVERY AND THE SOUTH 134
35. I'LL GET DRUNK WHEN ROOSEVELT DIES 140
36. MADISON SQUARE GARDENS 143
37. THE GREAT PARADE OF ALL THE IRISH 146
38. THE PICKETING OF THE WALDORF-ASTORIA 148
39. ARE AMERICAN TEENAGE GIRLS LIKE ENGLISH ONES? .. 153
40. A POSTCARD FROM LIMA 158
41. HERE THE BRITISH COME! 159
42. ATLANTIC CITY 168
43. SOUTH PACIFIC 171
44. DINNER WITH THE ROCKEFELLERS 174
45. CALIFORNIA DREAMING 178
46. A SAD DEPARTURE 181
47. COWBOY AND WESTERN 183
48. CALIFORNIA LIVING 188
49. SANTA BARBARA 191
50. THE TOP OF THE MARK 196
51. AN EMOTIONAL FAREWELL 199

EPILOGUE	201
PLEASE REVIEW AN ENGLISHMAN IN NEW YORK	203
ALSO BY SIMON MICHAEL PRIOR: THE COCONUT WIRELESS	204
ALSO BY SIMON MICHAEL PRIOR: THE SCENICLAND RADIO	206
ALSO BY SIMON MICHAEL PRIOR: THE POMEGRANATE BUSKER	208
PHOTOS TO ACCOMPANY AN ENGLISHMAN IN NEW YORK	210
ABOUT THE AUTHOR	211
ACKNOWLEDGEMENTS	213
WE LOVE MEMOIRS	214

INTRODUCTION

In 1948, at the age of 21, my father, John Miskin Prior, of Croydon, England, received a Rotary International grant to study post-graduate Economics and Sociology at Columbia University in New York. He sailed for New York in August 1948 and lived at International House in Manhattan until his return in July 1949. He also travelled extensively around the states of New York, New Jersey, and Pennsylvania, as well as further afield to the Central and West United States, speaking to Rotary clubs, and attending social functions.

He witnessed Truman's incredible victory over Dewey in the 1948 Presidential election, so unexpected; the newspapers were reprinted. He met and dined with John D Rockefeller Jnr. and his son John D Rockefeller III, Eleanor Roosevelt, her son Elliot Roosevelt, and his wife the actress Faye Emerson, as well as several other people occupying similarly privileged positions in society. He saw Humphrey Bogart and James Cagney at work making movies. He was one of the first people ever to see *Kiss me Kate*, *South Pacific*, and *Death of a Salesman*. He was interviewed on both American and Canadian Radio, and broadcast on ABC television. He met many American people who remained his lifelong friends.

This was at a time where Europe was just starting to recover from World War II, an event which hardly affected Americans' day-to-day lives at all. There are many references in John Miskin Prior's writing to America being the 'Land of Plenty' as against England's post-war rationing regime, with shortages of food and other essentials.

It is interesting to note John's conversion during the year from a staunch and proud Englishman, to being pro-American, open minded and worldly wise.

During his year in the US, he wrote lengthy letters weekly to his parents and his girlfriend. These were kept by the recipients, and eventually found their way to the author. In 2020, the letters were transcribed and edited to become these memoirs.

The reader should note that some expressions in these memoirs, for instance the use of the word *negroes*, are reflective of the era in which they were written, and are now considered offensive. *SMP*.

1. HURRICANE IN THE ATLANTIC

MOORE-McCORMACK LINES, INC.
5 BROADWAY -:- NEW YORK 4, N. Y.

26th August 1948 - 2nd September 1948

I am now safely aboard the Marine Juniper and berthed after a good train journey down to Southampton. My luggage did not get opened. I talked quite a lot to people on the train and I do expect the voyage will be quite jolly.

The Marine Juniper weighs 13,000 tonnes, its average speed is sixteen knots and it has 600 students aboard with about 300 crew. A better introduction to American life, food and students could not be imagined than this ship. It will probably be far more revealing and useful than a trip on the Queen Mary would have been so I had better try and tell you a little about it.

I was soon talking to the people with whom I had been sitting on the train to Southampton, being forced to intervene at some caustic comments on the English summer. I have had a good deal to do with them since. There are undoubtedly great advantages to be had from going on the Marine Juniper even though it was a bit like a youth hostel afloat so far as sleeping accommodation went. But the food has been simply marvellous. I have eaten each DAY, one week's meat ration, one week's bacon, two eggs and some poultry, together with a marvellous assortment of cooked vegetables, iced drinks, fruit, cheese, grapes, nuts, etc. It is far richer food than I have ever before tasted. We have breakfast at 7.30 a.m., lunch at 11.30 a.m., dinner at 5 p.m., and coffee and biscuits, known as *cookies* in America, at 10.50 p.m.

Being a student ship, there are programmes for returning Americans for discussion of their experiences, which they call 'evaluating', and programmes for European students going to the US called 'orientation'. Helping Americans to evaluate England and getting orientated myself takes up a good deal of time morning and afternoon! The efforts of the ships' leaders to orientate the poor Europeans were excellent and I landed in America knowing far more what to expect than I should have done had I gone on the Queen Mary. Several days we have square dancing which is an American cross of old time and folk dancing, and in the evenings films or more dancing. With the motion of the ship and whizzing around it is quite hectic I assure you. The leading light in all these activities is a young professor of history. In the meantime, we are able to walk and talk on deck and watch the mighty ocean.

I have met some remarkably interesting people, both male and female, conveniently situated in all parts of the States for a future tour. I have become friendly with the three girls with whom I sat going to Southampton, named Maeve McPeek, from Connecticut, Joan Perry from Boston, Ruth Yorke also from Boston and their friends Dick and Virginia Lee-Underwood from Oklahoma. I also met Kathleen Baird; an English girl teaching in Washington D.C. There were some Englishmen on board; a Reverend Harold Fife from Whyteleafe who was an interdenominationalist connected with the North Africa mission, Mr A D Walsh; a chemistry don at Cambridge, Jean White who is to study nutrition at Columbia University and has been a lecturer at Kings College, London, another girl going to do horticulture at California and a couple of men emigrating to the US.

Life on the Marine Juniper was an excellent introduction to American students and their ways. It initiated me into certain things which might have seemed inexplicable. I think one saw both the attractiveness of the American, particularly of his friendliness and some of those modern manners known collectively as 'dating' which appear to many, especially the Christian, as being harmful to the best development of personality; albeit it was most educational to take a walk round the ship about midnight! Many slept on deck as being cooler, but those who did so got a rich reputation, for the disused gun turrets were notoriously used. I did not sleep on deck obviously, for my reputation if nothing else.

There will doubtless be further comment on this as time goes, but I think it may be difficult to go dancing without getting into compromising situations unless one is careful. Of course, I shall want to go, but I do not intend becoming mixed up in the current American pattern of dating.

Meave McPeek (left) and either Joan Perry or Ruth Yorke (right) on the Marine Juniper. Photo: John Prior

The people I was with on the boat luckily thought the whole set-up ridiculous, one could therefore act as in England quite satisfactorily. In short although I think American University life will be somewhat different from English, I have no doubt I shall settle down. As far as I can judge generally their academic standards are lower than ours, but that applies more to undergraduate work than graduate, and explains why American graduates often take First Degrees like a BSc in England. Their standards of entry are not high and about half fall out before the end of their college days.

Everyone has been amazingly friendly, and I expect to visit some of them at various times. One slice of luck is that a teacher, who is a Rotarian from California, is in our cabin and he has said that if I would like to go to California, he will try to raise any extra money to pay the fare across America, which sounds altogether most promising.

The weather on the voyage was fair, and although the first few days were rough, I was healthy, and I felt no ill effects. But then we heard rumours of a hurricane off America, and last Wednesday we hit the edge of it. The winds were 50 miles per hour, the heat intense, the ship bumping helplessly about, and I regret to say I had to miss two meals. It was preceded by terrific humid heat and a pork lunch. All three combined to send me to my cabin from 5 p.m. Wednesday to 10 a.m. Thursday which was unfortunate. The rest of the time I felt quite all right, and in fact I greatly surprised the rest of our table when I did not appear. It was most unfortunate as I had hoped after weathering the first rough day to be able to cope with them.

The ship had a newspaper, which told us news of our progress and that we were sailing about 400 miles a day. This newspaper has given rise to a good deal of amusement, as has the loudspeaker system used for calling people to meals and for other announcements. Two gems are often heard: 'will the chief purser come to the purser's office' and 'will the chief steward go to the purser's office and the chief purser to the captain's cabin'; these in one breath.

I am now more than ever sure that I shall have a marvellous time, although I will be glad when I know exactly where I shall be living at Columbia University. I gather New York is really a most expensive place to live, but my scholarship is fairly generous, and I should manage all right. Haircuts are one dollar a piece (five shillings) – isn't that frightful – I shall let it grow.

I am really looking forward to landing early tomorrow morning. We shall spend tonight on deck watching New York approach.

2. AN UNWELCOME CUSTOMS INSPECTION

MOORE-McCORMACK LINES, INC.
5 BROADWAY   -:-   NEW YORK 4, N. Y.

4th September 1948

There was amazing excitement as we approached New York on Friday night. A whole lot of us were right forward in the bow, watching breathlessly for the first light from land which appeared at 8.20 p.m. It was a lightship, and then gradually the thousand lights of the Long Island shore and roads became visible until the sky was ablaze. It is hard to imagine a more tremendous spectacle than the gradual appearance of New York on the skyline. We reached the narrows of New York harbour, with the Statue of Liberty, and Manhattan with its huge skyscrapers grouped together twinkling with a myriad of lights looking like some great cathedral, and brightest and tallest of all being the Empire State Building.

We anchored between Staten and Coney Islands, and stayed there until morning. We had our usual tea, coffee, and biscuit pack with fruit we had judiciously collected, and retired at 12.30 a.m. to be up for breakfast at 6 a.m. Having our bags already packed, we prepared to dock at pier 95 at about 9.30 a.m., passing the Statue of Liberty symbolically clouded in mist, which was appropriate as we awaited a gruelling and ridiculous four hours from immigration and customs officials to enter the land of liberty.

The immigration people are most particular, and the customs inspection is a long chaotic process, with form filling on board, collection of the same in an enormous queue in the Customs House, and allotment of an inspector. The Americans are agreed the British way is infinitely superior. It is very, very hot. I do hope everything goes all right today. I shall be going to the Hotel Commodore.

3. DAZZLING NEON AND UNBELIEVABLE SKYSCRAPERS

6th September 1948

I am safely arrived in New York, and am still alive, though the traffic is naughty enough to drive and race on the wrong side of the road.

I am now at the Hotel Commodore, and today is Labour Day, the equivalent here of August Bank Holiday, so I have not been to see people at Columbia University yet. New York is easy to find one's way about in and very dazzling especially by night. The shops of course are a living marvel. The hotel is huge, and I should think equivalent to London's Grosvenor or The Savoy.

Once out of the dock everything went smoothly. I met Maeve McPeek's parents outside the pier, and they very kindly drove me to the hotel, as they had a car. There I soon found that my room was booked, and after checking in, the McPeeks took me out to lunch at the Castle Holme Restaurant, where we had a marvellous Swedish dish called *smörgord* which made a good introduction to New York for me. The McPeeks seem nice people; he is a professor of English, they live in Connecticut, and they have invited me to go and spend a weekend with them, which I shall do, as with several other people whom I meet on the Marine Juniper, or puddle jumper as it is affectionately known.

Following that I went back to the Commodore, and settled in. My room is number 1684 on the 16th floor. The price of the room here is $5.25 a night, about average for central New York, I think, and includes a private bathroom, which I have used extensively trying to keep cool in the shower. There is no food attached to the $5.25, and on the American pattern all that is paid for separately. The Commodore is on East 42nd Street by Grand Central Terminus, which is a palatial building making Waterloo seem like a poor country cousin. Apart from one dinner at $2.95 I have not eaten at the hotel at all, but at places where the food is certainly cheaper and tips etc can be kept reasonable. I received $10 from Rotary while on the boat, I was able to take the remaining $24 of the £7-10-0 I got from US lines off the boat so that was good, and I received another $50 Rotary money at the Commodore for weekend expenses.

On Saturday evening, I took my first real look around New York, going to 5th Avenue, looking at the Empire State Building, architecturally the finest as well as the tallest skyscraper, and I looked in shop windows, where not everything seemed desperately expensive, but more than utility price in most cases. Food is dearer than London, probably one third more. I also went to Times Square, and the famous part of Broadway where the cinemas are, the neon lighting is quite dazzling to the point of blinding.

I retired early after a bath and a shower and on Sunday I really saw and liked more of New York. I went to St Bartholomew's church in Park Avenue at 51st Street, to the 11 a.m. choral communion, a little opulently done I thought, although extremely low church. They had a choir of 24 ladies and 16 men singing for all they were worth, music more rousing than devotional. This was not ideal to me; I shall have to find a satisfactory church. St Bartholomew's is one of New York's richest churches right next to the Waldorf Astoria, and frequented by judges etc. After the service I went on a characteristically humorous conducted tour of the church, which is in the Byzantine style and heavily mosaiced and marbled.

On Sunday afternoon, I took a twenty-minute bus ride to the cathedral of St John the Divine at 112th Street and Amsterdam Avenue. It is incomplete, the nave and chancel are built, but a temporary roof and walls are placed where the transepts and central tower will be, and the western towers are not completed either. For evensong they had 24 men in the choir and normally there are also 50 boys, but they were on vacation. It was more congregational than an English Cathedral. The building I thought rather dull, ponderous, and dark, but they seem immensely proud of it. It is of course to be bigger than any other gothic cathedral, but lacks light and shade, and is not such good work as Truro or Liverpool Cathedrals in England. They have daily services, and the precentor was quite up to the mark.

I also took my first look at Columbia University from the outside. It stands on a small hill and covers a great deal of ground. The buildings are mainly red brick, and set out in courts. I returned to the centre of New York by way of Riverside Drive. New York city has five boroughs, Manhattan, Brooklyn, Richmond, Queens, and The Bronx. Of these Manhattan Island is the main centre, and contains all the famous buildings. The avenues are broad, and lined with skyscrapers and magnificent shops. The streets are narrower, but some are very important. 42nd Street where I am now is about equivalent to The Strand in London. In the evening I inspected the 170 pages of the New York Sunday Times and went to bed.

The next morning, I went to the Music Hall at the Radio City in the Rockefeller Centre, which is very famous, and of course the largest in the world. It was an excellent stage show celebrating the Golden Anniversary of the city of New York in brilliant dancing, singing, and spectacle. I also saw the film *A Date with Judy* and I watched the stage show twice. Afterwards I had a huge juicy salad and lettuce mayonnaise for lunch in the Promenade Restaurant of the Rockefeller Centre at the foot of the RCA building in The Plaza. It has fountains playing and a huge bronze statue of Wisdom Saving her Seed or something like that. During the afternoon I read and walked around the city a little.

Then on Tuesday I went to see Miss Ella Clark, at the Rotary office here. She is very charming and helpful, and she gave me the next cheque for $500 which will see me through for a little while.

On the whole Manhattan and the centre of New York are more attractive than I had expected. The skyscrapers make wonderful sights backed against each other and are just unbelievable, although everything is so tall that one does not always notice them quite so much, and all the straight streets add to this, as does the ever-present Hudson River. The shops are marvellous, although I do not anticipate having enough money to buy much extra, not yet a while at any rate. The food is of course exceptionally good, but you can easily spend more, and obtain poorer food than in London. The fabulous food is at fabulous prices and there are no subsidies, or 'five-shilling meal order' to keep the costs in check.

On the boat all were agreed on how well and fairly Britain's rationing worked. Apart from the Marine Juniper, however, I have not been able to compare Britain and America much. There is one bitter blow. The Americans do not have afternoon tea. They make no cakes other than Madeira variety, and are quite clueless about how to make or at what temperature to drink tea. They have three meals a day; breakfast; lunch; dinner, against our four.

I shall hope to be able to buy a few things before I come home, not everything is out of reach of my purse. A portable Remington typewriter is $65, of course the duty at Southampton would be terrific so I shall see if I can afford one. I am not immensely enticed by the ties, but the shirts and red pullovers are attractive. I shall buy nothing until I can do a little careful estimating of my expenditure.

4. A LUCKY BREAK

8th September 1948

I have had a very lucky break, and I can now tell you that my permanent address will be: International House, 500 Riverside Drive, New York, NY. Telephone: Monument 2-8500.

This is how it came about. I went to Columbia University yesterday only to find that my letter applying for a room had arrived just one minute before me. There was therefore no chance of a room in one of the halls of residence for this term, and I was advised to go either to International House, which is five minutes' walk from the university, or to try to get a room off campus. I went to the registry and was given some addresses of rooms including a highly recommended one, not thinking from what I had heard that there was a hope of accommodation so late at International House, which is in extremely high demand. However, I decided to go there anyway before investigating any of the off-campus options.

At International House, I was asked to fill in an application form and come back in the morning. I was informed that there was a fair chance of success because they allot rooms on a quota basis by nationality, and owing to the dollar shortage there were very few Englishmen there. This morning I returned and saw a Mrs Ford, who immediately fixed me up with a room and seemed very anxious for me to come.

The room is on the fifth floor, and I move in permanently at the end of next week, having a temporary room until then. The cost is $9.25 a week, with no meals, but it is not dear for New York, and cheaper than an off-campus room, about the same cost as a Columbia University on-campus hall room with of course far greater advantages.

Before accepting the room at International House, I sought advice from both the adviser to foreign students at the university and Miss Clark at New York Rotary. Miss Clark was most enthusiastic, and said I must be amazingly lucky, as International House is one of the most sought-after places in New York. And they accepted me without being on their waiting list or having letters of reference! I am naturally delighted, and I think from a social and economic point of view it may be even better than one of the halls at the university, where I might struggle to keep up with rich and gay Americans.

International House was built by John D. Rockefeller Jnr. in 1924. It stands on Riverside Drive just beyond Columbia University and is a fine building having 500 residents, and five public rooms, a cafeteria, various social functions, a barbers' shop and other facilities and it is of course a meeting place of all nations which is excellent. Everything about it seems very pleasant and I am sure there will be every opportunity for both work and play there, it even has a piano. I am convinced it will be so much better than living in an off-campus room. I am now off to have some lunch and then to get registered at the university.

International House, New York. Photo: John Prior

Excerpt from a 1948 brochure from International House
The citation information of this brochure from the 1940s is unknown.
Please advise if you are the author or know who they are.

5. NEWS OF AN EXCITING TRIP

500 RIVERSIDE DRIVE
NEW YORK 27. N.Y.

11th September 1948

I moved to International House on Thursday afternoon, but I am as yet only in a temporary room, though near where my permanent one will be. All the rooms are similar, and most convenient, containing a bed with a sprung mattress, a desk with drawers and pigeonholes at the back, a mirror, a bookcase, a chest of drawers, and large clothes cupboard for hanging suits etc. There is also an easy chair, a desk chair, a reading lamp, and a standard lamp. There will be plenty of room for all my possessions. There is one picture already, but I would have brought one of my own pictures had I known the kind of place I would be staying in.

Given the alternative of this room at $9.25 a week or an off-campus room in an apartment at $10.00, International House seemed to offer by far the best facilities, as the off-campus room provided no meals, and I would not be living with an American family as one might in England at all. So far as I can see, in America there are no board and lodgings as there are in England.

Living at International House will be a fine opportunity to meet people. It is around seven minutes' walk from the centre of Columbia University. This Morningside Heights part of New York, overlooking the Hudson River, seems quite the best. I am admitted at the university, but do not know my courses yet, and will probably have to make a few changes to my plans once I find out more about how they run things there.

I hope to get on one of Reinhold Niebuhr's courses at Union Theological Seminary as well, if the times work out.

I am only here until Monday morning, as then I leave with about twenty other foreign students for a tour of New York State arranged by Columbia University's adviser to foreign students and New York Rotary. We shall visit six centres, returning the following Sunday, staying with Rotarians overnight and having meals with them, and seeing under their guidance in the daytime the life, industrial or agricultural, of their respective neighbourhoods. It is a fine opportunity, and all this is for $25.00 which is probably less than it costs to live a week here, especially when there is nothing happening yet at the university. It will be a good break before term begins.

New York has been stupidly hot, but today is lovely following torrential rain yesterday.

Students on the steps of International House. Photo: John Prior

6. WONDERFUL SOCIAL INVITATIONS

500 RIVERSIDE DRIVE
NEW YORK 27, N.Y.

12th September 1948

I am now acquainted with everything at Columbia University. All was in order about my admittance, and now we await registration on the 20th and 21st. I then must see what courses to take. I was admitted to the sociology department because of studying under Professor Lynd. The MA here is not a great deal above BSc standard, and you attend several lecture courses, so I may go into the history department, where my subject seems to fit in better. Until I see Professor Lynd I cannot tell. I will explain how their system works when I know a little more, but there's much more red tape than in England and you pay for individual courses. You cannot, officially at any rate, go popping into other courses as one did in LSE *(London School of Economics where John studied an economics BSc – SMP)*. If I want to change courses, it can be done I gather. I am also thinking of taking one of Reinhold Niebuhr's courses at the Union Theological Seminary, which is situated between International House and Columbia University. I can do this simply by paying the requisite fee. But that depends on if the time allows.

I expect to save a good deal of money on laundry, as there is a washing machine and electric irons at International House, which only cost 25c to use. The English girl who is a lecturer at the Kings College of Household and Social Science, London, and who is doing a course at Columbia University, has instructed me on how to use the machine and iron. Laundry is so expensive; the official estimate is $80 for a year, and I'd far rather have the money for something else. I have washed and ironed five shirts; one pair of pyjamas; seven pairs of socks and four hankies all in two hours, with washing and drying machines and a regulated electric iron, which is one that can be kept at any temperature and does not keep getting hotter or colder. I do not think I have missed my vocation but may have added another competency! Precise directions on washing socks would be welcome as they don't go in the machine. At any rate I shall launder everything myself, except separate collar shirts, although I shall try these. This exercise was a great saving in dollars and quite fun; I almost held an exhibition of my work.

The food at Columbia University seems quite good, although I shan't know until after we get back from our week away as the cafeteria is closed. It is roughly speaking a third more expensive than in England. All the better restaurants, which serve the really marvellous food, usually charge as much as 15 to 25 shillings for food alone if you are to have significantly more than you can get in London. Although no student on a scholarship can enjoy all the food New York has to offer, there really is an amazing variety, and he can feed well. You can have milk at any meal, and eggs and meat are plentiful, unlike the dairy shortages in England.

I shall be able to use the deposit bank at Columbia University which is satisfactory, and leave money in the safe here, so that is settled.

On Thursday I went to the Rotary lunch. It was rather heartier and with more singing than I am used to, but the food at $2.25 (I did not pay) was melon, baked fish tomato and potato and apple pie, which would have cost three shillings in England. I was introduced to the President, and other officials, who were all very charming, and Miss Clark sat me next to a certain Consulting Engineer called George Diehl, under whose wing I believe I shall be. I am going to church with him tomorrow at the Little Church around the Corner (1 East 29th Street at 5th Avenue). He and an Englishman were most helpful in advising me about one or two things. They said I should hire evening dress; there is no need to buy it as I shouldn't need it much. I may try to get a typewriter but if not, there is one which may be rented by the half hour here at International House.

I have had some wonderful social invitations. This afternoon I am going on the Round Manhattan Steamer with Miss Hitchcock, a middle-aged schoolteacher I met on the boat. On the Marine Juniper I also met some French people who live in New York, and I have been invited to see them. Then this evening I will be going to the Pepsi Cola Centre International Lounge, probably with Jean White, the English lecturer here. British Subjects are required to register at the British Consulate, and while I was doing that, I was put in contact with some English people living near here and they will soon be inviting me to their home.

It is rather annoying not being able to unpack completely yet.

7. AN EXCITING TOUR OF NEW YORK STATE

500 RIVERSIDE DRIVE
NEW YORK 27, N.Y.

Sunday, September 19, 1948

The Rotary tour of New York state went off really well and we had a marvellous time. It was the first one of its kind to be arranged and was something of an experiment being part of Rotary's Home Study Tours Programme and the idea of Mr Troup Mathews, Columbia University's Adviser on Foreign Students, to get international students into American homes. His theory was that visiting students often lack the means to travel; the contacts to make it interesting; and the homes in which to stay. All these difficulties are overcome; there being in my mind two main disadvantages coupled with the obvious benefits. Firstly, that Rotarians come rather from one group, so far as politics and ideas go, and secondly, only the prosperous side of life is shown.

There were twelve of us from seven countries on the trip: England; Denmark; Finland; Iran; Israel; India and Belgium. We travelled by a chartered coach and visited Yonkers, just outside New York; Schenectady close to Albany; Johnstown and Utica, and the whole trip was so successful, both we and the Rotarians seem to think that it is a fine and practical idea for fostering international understanding, and for enabling students to see the homes and meet the people of America.

At Yonkers we had lunch with the Rotary club, and afterwards four of us made short speeches which seemed to please them. I briefly said what a good idea I thought it was for the Rotarians to have brought me to this land, and gave greetings from my home towns of Croydon and Wallington. Of the towns that we visited I should not say that Rotarians are invariably better off or higher up here; rather that all executive and neo-executive jobs are given more importance and are more highly paid. The meeting was boisterous, nay rowdy, under the direction of the Secretary, a school music director, who had the manner of a lion-tamer. He shouted jovially at everyone and never sat down once. When the guests were introduced, they all shouted "Hi ye Bill" or "Hi ye George" – he directing them. They sang Rotary songs, which he conducted and played for, rushing round the room forcefully upbraiding those whose mouths were not working vigorously!

In the afternoon we visited the largest carpet factory in the world, Alex Smith, which was remarkably interesting. That night I stayed with the Director of Education, Mr Willis. He entertained with a dinner that was so huge with vast slices of beef that I was near bursting. Another boy was staying opposite, and each house had an eligible daughter, the one in mine being called Rachel. After dinner we went out in the other girl's open-top car and drove around for an hour. We got lost, I think, though this is rigorously denied. Then we went to another house where, with the boy staying there, we had a drink, which was most enjoyable. All the cars are those large ones, and this Hollywood presentation of people hopping in and driving off at great speed is realistic.

The following day we visited Franklin Delano Roosevelt's home at Hyde Park, and saw everything there. Roosevelt was hated by the businessmen as a rabid socialist, a diabolical cross of Aneurin Bevan, Shinwell and Hugh Dalton. He should not be mentioned in a Rotary business household! But no Rotarian will explain whether there was any alternative to what Roosevelt achieved in 1933-40. Of course, Rotarians are not typical, but Roosevelt has more enemies here it seems than Churchill has in England, perhaps because he was in power many years pre-war. At Schenectady I stayed with a doctor and again was forced to overeat. We went over the General Electric Works and had a good lunch there. It was interesting to note that works canteens are not compulsory here.

Then we travelled on to Johnstown, which is an old country town with a glove making and tanning industry over which we looked. It was founded by one Sir William Johnson, an 18th Century Irishman who was clearly most amazing. At the Rotary lunch there we again made speeches and I caused some amusement by saying they were a more gracious club than Yonkers, doubtless because the town was founded by a gracious Irishman. I then was just able to congratulate them on having adopted as an experiment Croydon's method of selection of seats at tables for lunch; they thought it would be a good way of mixing up people. I stayed with a box maker aged 80, a remarkable old fellow.

On to Utica, a beautiful drive up the Mohawk valley, where I lodged with a lawyer and his wife named Mr and Mrs Heber Griffith. They took me out to a golf club, where I had a huge sirloin steak. I caused some amusement when I said I chose to abstain from fish while I could; the Americans I gather regarding *sea-food*, as they call it, very highly. We then went to see *The Best Years of our Lives*.

In the morning we went for a general tour of Utica and then to the Rotary lunch where the speaker was a Republican giving a non-political speech whose ideas were incredibly antediluvian. I quite enjoyed it. While in Utica several of us were interviewed in a radio programme, and I have therefore now been broadcast. I answered questions about food rationing and demonstrated the quantity of meat ration by saying my previous night's steak was larger than the English meat ration for a whole week. This subsequently appeared in the papers as '*Mr Prior has eaten more good food in America in days, than in English rations in months*'; which is not my experience, since I have a limited number of dollars. I think it was successful, and I am told I sounded quite natural by my hostess there, who listened in and has since written to me.

The people's hospitality and kindness were remarkable, and what food! The streets in the better off neighbourhoods are most attractive, and in all the towns in which we stayed they were tree-lined, with gleaming white Houses built mainly of wood with grass all around, though no elaborate gardens and no fences. The rooms are usually so large and arranged *en-suite*, leading one from the other, with good sized halls and kitchens.

All the bathrooms are fitted with showers, which are a twice-daily necessity here so far due to the heat. Their kitchens seem also to be extremely well-equipped in every respect. The scenery in New York State is certainly delightful, ranging from mountains and wooded areas to the beautiful Mohawk Valley, but the Hudson River from New York to Albany takes some beating, with its cliff sides, and the Catskill Mountains in the background.

Our chartered coach was most comfortable, and we arrived back in the city on Friday evening at 8.30. So ended a most enjoyable trip.

Today after church, playing the piano, reading the huge Sunday paper, and writing thank you letters to my hosts on the tour, I went to a tea for newcomers here and talked until after 11 p.m. with those I met.

I am now in the process of completing registering at Columbia University, having seen about five professors yesterday all of whom were charming. Tomorrow we are greeted by Eisenhower at the Opening Exercises, followed by an address on *The University and Society*.

I am happily unpacked and settled in my permanent room at International House. Everything fits in beautifully, and my books are colourful. The activities here will I think be marvellous, and such interesting people. The food is really incredibly good.

8. A PRESENTATION FROM EISENHOWER

500 RIVERSIDE DRIVE
NEW YORK 27, N.Y.

22nd September 1948

The Presidential Campaign is now getting underway with Mr Truman 'giving 'em hell', to use his own words, and Mr Dewey confining himself to pious hopes, and guarantees to do what his party has not been doing for the past two years in the congress where they have a majority; a fact Truman emphasises. It appears Dewey will be elected, though there may be a democratic Senate which would be interesting. It is very much a choice, as the papers say, between Tweedledee and Tweedledum.

    Last Saturday four of us had lunch with Troup Mathews of Columbia University, and discussed arrangements for a further trip going to Massachusetts or Connecticut possibly at Thanksgiving time (which is at the end of November) for three or four days, this would be very good, as the trip to upstate New York was so successful.

    On Sunday I went to communion at the Cathedral, and then to the Riverside Church, which adjoins here, and was built by Rockefeller for Dr Fosdick the great preacher. The service was non-conformist, and fully musical, the choir consisted of 34 females with 16 men.

They are paid quite well I think, like all New York choirs, though the services still sound too much like a hearty choral society with spoken or prayerful intermission. On Sunday afternoon there was a welcoming tea to newcomers here at International House, and various of us talked after that until quite late. On Monday and Tuesday, I registered at the university, and today I did laundry and attended the Opening Exercises.

I went to see Professor Lynd on Monday morning, and he was certainly most charming. He is about 55 years old, medium height and build, grey hair, and glasses. He seemed most pleased to see me; and he said immediately that he thought my idea of doing some history made sense. Seeing that I was here for only a year; that it was a travelling scholarship; and that I wanted to get the best possible picture of America past and present; he suggested that I should go through the courses listed under Economics, Sociology, History and Government with him, pick out those I was interested in; then go and see the professors concerned in their various departments; emphasize that I was here for only a year and hope they would let me in.

He also asked if I was going to take a degree, to which I replied that I intended doing so. He then said he wondered whether it would be the best use of my time to do so. He thought I would gain more by doing varied courses, reading and miscellaneous travel, and visiting as I saw fit, rather than by just taking a degree course, all of which presumes a knowledge of how the American degree system works. To get a bachelor's degree takes four years, two of which are occupied in general work in English Foreign Language, Science, Social Science etc; and in the last two there is some specialisation. The Master's degree is not a research degree, and you attend courses for it, and write an essay. Therefore, it is still on the lines of our bachelor's degree, and is not much of a higher standard.

Then the system of marking is different. Each course is a certain number of points, usually three, and you are either tested as you go along, or by terminal exams. By these means eventually you are graded. To get a master's degree you must take thirty points, nine of which are given for attendance only; then there is a small exam in May, and you have to write an essay for it. Thus, whereas in England you get your degree and class in a few hours one June, here you get it all along, and you cannot miss lectures as we were able to, without a pass at all.

To take a degree you also must be within a department, and you work on whatever courses permitted that you wish to take. But you must remain within the department. This is somewhat of a restriction. I had anticipated getting the degree by thesis and doing what work and courses I liked. But here you pay for the individual course and not for the term as a whole, thus you cannot flit from one to the other. If I were registered for an MA in either history or sociology, I could not do the general work on American history and culture which Columbia University offers. I want to take two courses in the economics department: one on American economic history and a seminar in it; one in the history department; two in the sociology department; and one in the government department. That makes six courses in all. I should only take officially five, making a full fifteen points (three points a course) programme as I should take for a degree.

I saw Professor Brebner, who being himself English, advised me on what I should do. He thought my time would be wasted confining myself to a degree, which is not academically wanted much in Britain, being hardly higher than a bachelor's. I also saw Professor Commager, a nice little fellow who thought I would do well to range widely and get the broadest view I could of American history and life today, encountering as many different approaches as possible and getting to know as many professors as possible. With Professor Commager I shall do a course called 'Colloquialism in American Civilization since 1890', which should be excellent. Professor Goodrich (American Economic History Course and Seminars) said he would be delighted to have me in his course and thought my comparative knowledge with Britain would be invaluable.

Professor McMahon gives a course named 'The Federal System' in the spring session and one called 'The Political Setting of Public Administration' this session, which are useful lights on the American scene and in the government department. I went and saw him; he thought it an excellent idea to spend the year getting the maximum of information and he said, "come to my lectures and even if you don't, come and see me as I should like to know some things about Britain today."

Then with Professor Lynd, I shall do a course on 'Power in American Society' and also possibly a course named 'Basic Methods of Social Research' by a Miss Kendall. This latter is uncertain, and I can change my registration for any of these courses until October 9th, or decide to take the degree until then.

What it amounts to is these five professors who I saw and explained my case to all said, "do the wider work, and find out just what you can during your year here," and all thought the value of a degree would be far outweighed by the restriction I should have upon my work. As it is I shall do just what I had hoped: a year's study of America, not in books only, but also in travel and visiting. I can change my mind, but I think with this wealth of advice and the obvious advantages, I shall do as Professor Lynd and the others so unanimously advise.

I shall see Miss Clark, and then write to Rotary International about it, but they do not know anything, beyond that I wish to study something on American history, and I'm sure they will approve. Professor Lynd will write to them if necessary. Professor Commager said he had recommended several bodies giving this kind of travelling scholarship, not to require degrees, as real research was not possible in one year and a broad graduate study was preferable.

I shall still work on Beale's subject, probably in Prof Goodrich's course, and may write an essay on it because it is very interesting. Goodrich was a founder of the International Labour Office. Of course, in England, I should have done research in that subject of Anglo-US relations in social matters in the 19th Century and got a degree on that basis, but that can't be done here. Everything is most complicated visa office-like. However, I have now finally completed registration and have paid $160 fees, pending receipt of an interim cheque from Rotary International before paying the other $150.

I am most excited about everything, particularly about starting university tomorrow, and have been exercising in the traditional manner in my room, though lightly in deference to the man below. I have courses as follows:

- Monday 10.00 Professor Barzam: European Culture in the 19th Century. (I may listen to this but not officially taken)
- Monday 4:10 – 6.00 Miss Kendall: Basic Methods of Social Research. Fayerweather building
- Tuesday 9.00 – 6.00 Professor Goodrich: American Economic History. Fayerweather building.
- Tuesday 2:10 – 4.00 Professor Goodrich: American Economic History Seminar. Business Building.
- Wednesday 10.00 Professor Barzam: European Culture in the 19th Century. Fayerweather building.
- Wednesday 2:10 – 4.00 Professor Commager: Colloquialism in American Civilisation. Hamilton Building.
- Thursday 9.00 Professor Goodrich: American Economic History. Fayerweather building.
- Thursday 10.00 – 11.50 Professor Lynd: Power in American Society. Fayerweather building.
- Thursday 2.10 Professor Commager: American Constitutional History. Schermerhorn (possibly)
- Thursday 7.30 – 9.10 Professor McMahon: Political setting of public administration. Fayerweather building.
- Friday – free: good for weekends or visits to places of historic interest or museums etc.

I am still trying to see whether I can fit in a Reinhold Niebuhr lecture, but it would cost $30 at least. What I should like to do would be just to sit in incognito, or unofficially, and on Friday I shall try to see if I can manage anything through the University Chaplain, but the time element may prevent it.

Today the Opening Exercises were exceptionally good. I was lucky and sat quite close to the front. We sang the National Anthem, had a prayer, a greeting by the President, an address by Dr Edmund de Schweinitz Brunner on 'The University and Society', the hymn 'Stand Columbia', to the tune of 'Praise the Lord, ye heavens adore Him', and a Benediction. There was a procession in and out of fully robed professors, and Eisenhower was robed. He is just like his pictures, and has a merry smile most of the time, a sort of bemused twinkle when people clap him. He welcomed everybody by pointing out the opportunity which life and Columbia University offered to those who looked courageously for it.

On Monday night, the new people here at International House were officially welcomed by the director, Mr John G Mott, son of Dr John Mott, the great ecumenical churchman prominent at Amsterdam. Previously I had been introduced to Mr Mott by Roger Mastrude, the Education Officer, who seems I think to believe I shall be useful in discussion groups here. Then today Mrs Mott, who is Executive Secretary of the Greater New York Council for Foreign Students, rang me up and said that Mr Mastrude had suggested my name to her as a student likely to be good in helping with a new venture under the 'Carrie Chapman Cott Memorial Fund', to plan a programme of education for foreign students in the field of governmental responsibility in the US. The committee contains influential people and two other students from International House are going, so this looks like an opportunity to be in the centre of something important. The exploratory meeting is tomorrow night at 1010 Fifth Avenue, the very posh part, at the home of a Mrs Chas B Hemming. They seemed very keen that I should go, thinking I would have a lot to contribute, given my general interest in seeing the US and comparing it with Britain.

On Saturday afternoon I am going to Bakerfield, at the top end of Manhattan, to see Columbia University play football against Rutgers. This they do with great pomp and ceremony, with marching bands playing. Their football is a version of rugger. Then in the evening I shall be dining with those French people I met on the boat.

I think the money will work out well, because the food is good here, and will not average more than $2 a day for plenty. I have still bought nothing.

One little note: as you probably will have realised, the Americans show off, publicise or exhibit nothing to which they cannot apply a superlative of some kind. The largest, oldest, widest, newest, most hygienic, greatest, prettiest, any adjective will do, provided it suggests that it is the best of its class.

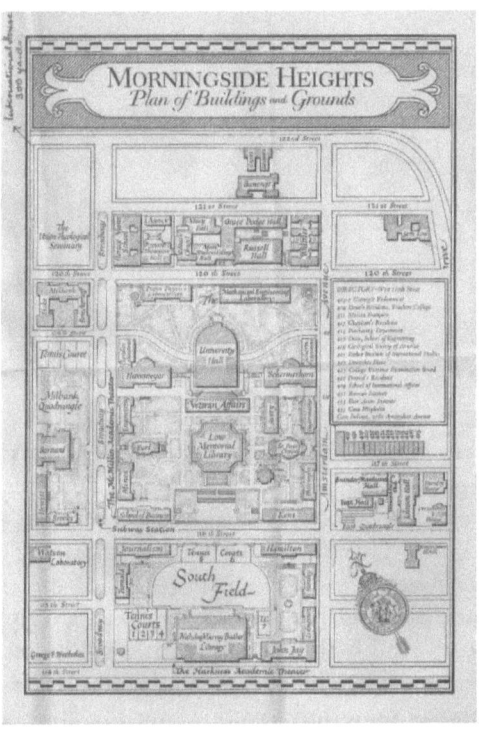

Excerpt from a brochure about Columbia University.

The citation information of this brochure from the 1940s is unknown. Please advise if you are the author or know who they are.

9. AMERICAN FOOTBALL

500 RIVERSIDE DRIVE
NEW YORK 27. N.Y.

Monday 27th September 1948

To say one likes New York is a bit difficult; it is a fascinating, even a gripping place; extreme poverty matched by fabulous wealth; areas as diverse as can be, whole foreign sections resplendent with their own newspapers. The skyscrapers and modern buildings are immensely impressive, and the sham gothic of the cathedrals and churches is not pleasing aesthetically (nor spiritually), and I wish there were a cathedral built more in spirit with the rest of the great buildings. Morningside Heights is a pleasant district; it has no skyscrapers and is quite airy overlooking the river and Riverside Park, although one is in the city, one is not in the popular stereotype of New York and Manhattan.

I will describe American university life when I am better able to judge it. But I have just provoked an American into saying that; if our undergraduate system of little set work week by week really works; it must need remarkably mature people. I agree with this but can hardly use it in argument.

I went last Thursday to a meeting of the University Christian Association, which is affiliated to the Student Christian Movement.

I discovered that it was a reunion of last year's members to formulate policy and mainly undergraduate, however the discussion was interesting. Getting posters printed seems a universal bane of the movement.

While I was there, I met the University Counsellor to Protestant Students, and was told by him that Union Theological College would probably let me sit in one of Reinhold Niebuhr's courses provided there is room. He will let me know on Wednesday. There is also a graduate session at Columbia University, which the chaplain's department organises and which I shall be able to attend. There is at Columbia University a building known as Earl Hall, which is the religious centre of the university, with a nicely furnished lounge. The University Christian Association seems strong and active, and has social and square dancing monthly. I shall join in their activities as I see fit, particularly if they are discussing Amsterdam, because the clergy like Dr Sochenan, who have wealthy New York churches, must explain how the World Council of Churches could condemn capitalism.

My two comments on the matter are:

1. If it causes depressions and therefore untold human misery, of course we must try to improve it.
2. If the minister is paid directly by his congregation, how much freedom of speech can he have?

There will also be general discussions at International House, and I am involved in the planning of these.

The chapel at Columbia University has a dome and short nave, apse and transepts. It also has a magnificent organ like the marvellous baroque ones in Holland after which it was modelled. The interior is in brick but quite pleasing. They have Holy Communion on Tuesday, Wednesday, and Thursday at 8 a.m. There is also a daily service at noon of varied type plus Sunday Holy Communion at 9 a.m. and morning service at 11 a.m.

Last Sunday I managed to arrive an hour early at 8 a.m. – was I mad? I had retired at 4 a.m., after visiting the French couple whom I saw on the boat. The time just flew by, as we talked with their friends, a professor of English, and his wife, and played various kinds of poker, though not for money. They live in West 63rd Street and are middle-aged. I shall be visiting them again.

Previously on Saturday, I visited Bakerfield to see the Columbia University football team play Rutgers and beat them 27-6. American football is different from ours. A team has eleven players, and four attempts in one 'down' to advance an aggregate of ten yards. If this is done, they have another 'down' and so on. If the ball passes to the other side or the yards are not made, then the other side has a 'down'. They have gangs of cheer leaders, who perform acrobatic feats of jubilation or disgust, and brass bands parading at intermission, who back up the respective sides. Altogether it was rather a thrilling experience and I was glad to attend. Eisenhower was there.

There is a magnificent record library here, to which I belong, and can therefore play records. One lovely one I've heard is *The Virgin's Slumber Song* by Max Reger; an old German folk song. It is sung by a soprano or contralto and the melody is mystic. I also play the piano occasionally after breakfast, and before church on Sundays, when there is no one about, but I really cannot play when there are other members of International House in the room. It is the only thing which really embarrasses me or makes me nervous.

So far as I know I still exert charm by the purity of my English accent, and resolutely refuse to praise all things American!

10. AMERICANS HAVE NO CONCEPT OF THE WAR

500 RIVERSIDE DRIVE
NEW YORK 27, N.Y.

4th October 1948

The news has not been at all eventful really, except in Paris, where it now seems that the Russians are:

a. Definitely stalling, and probably sincerely want agreement;
b. Want us to break off relations in some way, for their propaganda purposes.

The situation is bad, and I am sure that neither side can be pleased. Here I think communism is feared more than war, the Americans having experience of neither. I do not think most Americans have many ideas of what a modern war is like. I noticed that my accounts of living in air raids were received with surprise, rather than confirmation of what they had already heard. And I think that the fact that all are losers in modern war is unrecognised here.

I do not think anyone would so willingly think of war as do many Americans and the Press, had they any experience of it. I have seen no mention of the destruction and suffering it would cause, only a discussion of the Atom Bomb. Although it is idealistic, I think if statesmen thought in terms of human suffering instead of their country's prestige or pride, they might sometimes make better decisions. At any rate, morally we shall be in the wrong if we do not take Russia's latest overtures seriously, however much our leaders may think it's hopeless.

To return to more mundane matters, the last week saw me beginning work and enjoying classes and lectures very much, although they are quite different from England. They have lectures interspersed with questions, which we do not have so very much in England. I am just now off to a class in 'Modern Ideas of the State', with Professor McIver. Professor Commager is particularly good, so is Professor Lynd. I think I shall be busy with reading, and my normal pattern of activity fast filling in, so that there will be a close resemblance to my time at the London School of Economics.

I have been successful in getting on to Reinhold Niebuhr's lecture course on the 'Christian View of History'. He is a marvellous lecturer, and I may be able to imitate him come the time. His lecturing manner is like his public speaking. I shall hope to meet him personally at one of his open houses.

I have now received all the Rotary money I shall have until January 10th. I much prefer to have it in a lump sum, as I found that not unduly extravagant last year. I have deposited it at the Student Bank. I think I shall be able to manage, though not with very much money to spare. I have taken out an insurance health policy, covering outpatient and hospital treatment. I asked Mr Diehl's advice and he said insurance is a must. It cost $19.68, which is cheap, and is arranged by Columbia University. As he said, I might have an accident and then that would cost far more.

There are such a lot of nice people at International House, and always some dancing and discussing going on, if you do not wish to work. I have great fun with Americans, as I know enough now of America to be able to debate effectively with them, and I can usually swiftly think of replies. I have been elected to the International House Dormitory Council, and last Thursday at a party, I did a rather funny little speech in presenting a queen to her king and prospective husband, during a game. I did it in flamboyant official language, and have been receiving congratulations ever since. They seemed to appreciate it as being authentic English. I think I might try to get a mock trial arranged here; they are such fun.

I went to see the Italian film *Paisan* last Saturday night, with a couple of American fellows. Then on Sunday I went to the Union Theological Seminary in the morning and heard the president, Prof H P van Dusen, speak, followed by the Riverside Church again with people from International House. The main minister Dr Robert J McCracken preached, and they sang an anthem by E J Moeran and *The Spirit of the Lord* by Elgar.

On Sunday evening I went and saw those people to whom I was introduced by the British Consulate. They are English and named Ross. They took me to dinner with some relations, and we had an interesting evening. We talked about some old books on England which they have. The Rosses, who live next door to International House, have an Elizabethan play reading fortnightly that I shall attend. They are musical and theatrical. Their son had just missed getting the policeman's part in *Edward my Son*.

I met Rev. Daniel Jenkins, assistant editor of the Christian Newsletter. He is studying for a year at Union and we shall meet again, I knew him at the London School of Economics. The writer Alexander Miller is also here, and I have met him. He is well known in Student Christian Movement circles. During the week I started reading American history, the biography of Rockefeller, and other things of interest.

This coming weekend I hope to be going to stay with Maeve McPeek and her parents in Connecticut, provided they get some more rain; they have hardly any water left in Connecticut. It will be a good opportunity to see a bit of New England, and it is wonderful to see and visit as many people as possible. I continue to take the greatest care of myself and am still blissfully English. I think I may say, "sometime else," and, "surely," instead of, "yes," but that is all!

I am just off to get tickets for Eisenhower's installation.

11. A WEALTHY CONNECTICUT FAMILY

500 RIVERSIDE DRIVE
NEW YORK 27. N.Y.

11th October 1948

I have had a most enjoyable weekend in Connecticut, staying with the McPeeks. I took the 3.30 on Friday afternoon from Grand Central Terminal, and I was met at Hartford Station by the McPeeks at 6 p.m. We arrived at their house at Storrs after an hour's drive. Maeve McPeek's father is Professor of English at the University of Connecticut, which is a State University and in the country at Storrs. He is a published author, and is currently writing two books. The McPeeks have a nice little house right off the road on a fifty-acre plot of wood and meadowland with a high hill and a river. Their house is not large, though it has a good-sized living room, tastefully furnished which I like because it's good for parties! It is wholly delightful in every respect. The size of the grounds is not so exceptional here as it would be in England, as land is much more plentiful, and there is not so intensive development as there is in the English countryside. They are genuinely nice people with lots of particularly good conversation. On Friday evening after delicious food, Maeve and I went to a reception and dance at the university which was enjoyable.

The following morning, we all drove around the university and its campus which is being rapidly developed. They are currently building dormitories with huge concrete block walls of a new kind. It is pleasantly situated with quite attractive buildings, though in various 'Ye Olde' styles. The hilly country all around is well-wooded, almost uncleared forest really, which with rich autumn tints was a very magnificent sight.

In the afternoon we went to see Old Sturbridge Village in Massachusetts, a reconstruction of a typical New England village with its arts and crafts, displayed as it would have been in about 1810.

Then we had an excellent dinner at the 'Publick House', and so home to Storrs. On Sunday we went to church and heard the encyclical read, following by meeting the rector and his wife. The nearest church to Storrs is at Windham Centre some fifteen miles away, so quite a drive. In the afternoon we walked again, and then had tea to which several other people were invited. I left on the 7.22 p.m. from Hartford.

Tonight, there will be great excitement, as the Dormitory Council of which I am a member, is to be televised at 6.15 in the Home Room here. I do not know anything else yet, except that we shall be interviewed and talk about the work of the House. I shall therefore have both been broadcast and been televised. Then after that there will be the first play reading that I am going to, which should be most enjoyable.

Last Wednesday, we had a meeting to arrange the graduate seminar for people interested in theology. I talked a great deal, as I never can keep silent, and always seem to have ideas. I am working quite hard, reading a lot, and enjoying the classes. Professor Commager and I have frequent discussions in his class on his comparisons of English and American customs, but I always try to find incongruities in America if any are suggested in England.

The presidential election is becoming even more lively. I think the most sensible people fear both a Dewey victory and a Truman one. Dewey is so unattractive and only utters sugary sentiments, and is generally thought to be just a careerist who means to be President. People think in policy that he will be easily influenced by those special interests of which Truman speaks. On the other hand, Truman is not really a competent enough man, well-meaning as he may be.

His strongest point is that if the Republican Party believes in its platform, it could have carried it out when he asked it to during the life of the 'notorious 80th do-nothing Congress', instead of reversing all his requests.

This is rather why the Conservatives were defeated in 1945; because when they had had power, they didn't carry out their programme. The deadliest argument against the Conservatives was that if they believed in their platform, they could have brought it all in their twenty-odd years of power from 1919-1939.

Dewey's worst proposal is that the peace time uses of atomic energy should be developed by private enterprise, which would give them far too much power in the minds of sensible people. If ever there was a need for government enterprise it is in that field, so that its management may be publicly accountable to the people.

But Truman has not a united party or talented advisers, and in general though his speeches are vigorous, and he is *folksy* (homely), wherever he goes, he still seems to be certain to have a new home in January.

The past week's classes and lectures continued to be particularly good, and the common conversation or discourse 'Colloquialism in American Civilisation since 1890', with Professor Commager, is really most amusing, because he is always seeing if his comparisons of USA with Britain are thought valid by me, and he was of course at Cambridge last year. I am going to do a comparative study of the Government's attitude to developing industrialism in USA and Britain for Professor Goodrich's 'Education pertaining to seed' seminar, which will I think become interesting. It will I suppose be a long essay. I am going to do the course in 'Basic Methods of Social Research', with Miss Kendall for a term, as Professor Lynd thinks it will be useful.

Last Tuesday, there was the first discussion group and talk at International House with one Stringfellow Barr, he spoke on 'Europe at the present time'. On Wednesday, we had a meeting to arrange the Graduate Seminar of the University Council for Protestant Students. It will meet fortnightly on Wednesday evenings. Then on Thursday, there was folk dancing here, which was enjoyable. We are now beginning to make preparations for the Hallowe'en festival on October 30th. Each national group does something.

The English are going to do a piece on Sherlock Holmes in *The Murder at the Music Hall*, which will enable us to use most of our talent. We will be singing, acting and also performing a male ballet, probably *Three Little Girls from School are we*. I may sing *The Stately Houses of England*, which I have here.

Tomorrow is Eisenhower's installation, for which I have a ticket, and which begins at two o'clock. I think the most impressive thing will be the academic procession. The day is a university holiday, so there will be time for a good deal of reading, and I shall probably try to see a film in the evening.

I have bought a rather nice McPherson tartan tie in crushless material. There is a marvellous selection in all the shops although I do not care for the jazzy ones.

The weather is now mightily improved, and is a reasonable temperature with cold nights, but up till a few days ago it was extremely hot. Nearly all the people in Columbia University, International House, and New York in general, seem to wear the new look or length, so I wonder if England will have changed by the time I return.

12. THE BEST INTERVIEWEE ON ABC TV

500 RIVERSIDE DRIVE
NEW YORK 27, N.Y.

Columbus Day, 12 October 1948

Today is a university holiday in honour of Eisenhower's installation. The installation exercises were great fun. The arena was the whole area between the Low and Butler Libraries with a street running across. I sat in South Field and the installation itself was by Alma Mater Statue. This was surrounded by cypress trees and there were gold and blue banners between the Low Library columns. There were stands for distinguished guests and the whole area was filled with seats for people. The ceremonies began with military music, *Here comes the Bride* (!) and *Carmen*, followed by the academic procession, with heads of visiting and foreign universities entering after the Columbia University choir. Then came the faculty followed by the trustees, and Eisenhower and the mace preceding the Chairman of the Trustees. After the procession had slowly wound its way to the front of Low Library (named after a former President, as is the Butler library) there was the national anthem, and a prayer.

Then representatives of students, alumni and faculty briefly welcomed Ike. The Chairman of the Trustees presented the keys, and Ike gave his address. This was followed by the university hymn, *Stand Columbia*, and the benediction and a recessional during which Ike was almost mobbed!

The whole show was most impressive, particularly for Americans who do not have regal pageantry as do we.

The televising of the Dormitory Council at International House was most successful. It was a half hour show, and they had us sitting in the House room while we were interviewed, and various groups sung and played. The ABC people were delighted, and everyone congratulated me afterwards saying how well I had done, several said I was quite the best, and asked how long I had studied television etc. This was from those who make the actual television, as well as from those in the room.

After that, the play reading was good, and I was similarly complimented. I usually manage to amuse people somehow, particularly by comments on the American and English ways of life. Two things of mine are now classical. My comment on seeing the Manhattan skyline the first night that New York was sizeable. And a long definition of the difference between a pie and a tart in England, and a pie in USA and in Great Britain, which we had hysterics over one lunch time.

In more mundane matters, in our Hallowe'en thing I am to be the hero, an English lord in love with a chorus girl in the gay nineties.

13. THE DANCE OF THE SEVEN VEILS

500 RIVERSIDE DRIVE
NEW YORK 27, N.Y.

18th October 1948

I have become famous here as the result of the television interview, owing to one remark uttered in my naive voice. The interviewer was leading up to the major statement that International House is a difficult place to get into, and I replied quite honestly and innocently to his question, "Well no, not really, they seemed quite pleased to have me." That fairly brought the house down, and I have been hearing about it ever since. I think I was quite a highlight of the show from what I gather.

I have had a troublesome rash on my hand, so I went to the medical service at Columbia University last week, and I saw two doctors there, one a skin specialist. They gave me some Vioform ointment and vitamin A tablets. That was last Wednesday, and it is already practically well, so I hope it remains so.

Classes and lectures continue to go very well, and I like them all very much, which is a good thing. There are now quite a group of us who are friendly and can go out together enjoyably. Last Thursday evening we went to hear Marcel Dupre, the great French organist, give a recital in St Thomas Chapel, at 60th Street and 3rd Avenue.

It was very enjoyable, and the building was packed full of people, though he did not play enough Bach for my liking. Then last Friday, I went with others to Mr and Mrs Mott's home for tea.

On Saturday we went to the Museum of Modern Art in the afternoon, which had various peculiar products of the human mind and hand perpetrated recently for our delectation. It was really quite interesting, and we had great fun guessing what they were!! We also saw an old Greta Garbo silent film from 1927, presented as a kind of museum piece.

In the evening we went to a marvellous French-Spanish restaurant named La Bilbania, in Greenwich Village, which is in downtown on 14th Street at 7th Avenue. Greenwich Village is the New York equivalent of Soho and Chelsea. There we had for 95c; unlimited hors d'oeuvres; Galacian soup; salad; an entrée of kidneys; rice; chipped potatoes; and to follow fruit salad and ice cream and coffee! That is really cheap and the four of us capped it by having a bottle of Californian Burgundy, which was only $1.50.

On Sunday I went to Holy Communion at 9 a.m. and followed that by hearing Reinhold Niebuhr preach at Union Theological Seminary. The church was packed, and he preached on the theme about the peace of Babylon as an analogy of the UN and the peace of Jerusalem, being the World Government (Jeremiah 29) and warned people about expecting quick results from either. It was most impressive. Many from International House went, so there was plenty to talk about over lunch. It was an analysis of the place of 1948 in the general scheme of things, and how we were in captivity: ideas of corporate guilt, repentance etc.

Then in the afternoon I went with Bob Wallace from California, Bob Andress from Alabama and Curtis Green from Georgia to get tickets for the opera by Richard Strauss, then a repeated excellent visit to the restaurant, Bilbania, and we followed that by seeing English folk dancing in the Rockefeller Plaza in the UN festival there.

In the evening we saw the opera *Salome*, at the City Centre. It is a one-act opera; the music being splendid all through and the action interesting. It is the story of how Salome, Herodias's daughter, loves the captain of the guard, sees John the Baptist in prison, and then consents to perform the *Dance of the Seven Veils* for Herod in his lust in return for anything she may desire, which is the head of John on a silver platter.

The dance is quite startling, as she divests herself of the seven veils in turn, throwing off the last one as she falls at Herod's feet. These operas at the City Centre are excellent and tickets can be easily obtained, so I shall be going again.

This week we shall be beginning our preparations for Halloween with a vengeance.

There is an Australian girl from here coming to London. Her name is Sybil Wiley, and she is a very capable singer, having won the chief Australian voice scholarship, the Melba. She is hoping to get professional work in London. I do not think she knows many people in England.

International House Students in a park in New York. Photo: John Prior

14. YOU MAY NOT HAVE A GIRL IN YOUR ROOM

500 RIVERSIDE DRIVE
NEW YORK 27, N.Y.

Sunday October 24th, 1948

Really there seems as many things to do each day as there are storeys in the Empire State Building. The great new temptation here is talking in each other's rooms at night, after having finished a Coca-Cola in the Waffle Wing (no waffles, quite English!), at 11.15 p.m. We manage to combine intelligence with gaiety without dissipation! I am glad to be friendly with a group of Americans so that I get to know a little of how they think, and they come from Alabama and California so have quite different backgrounds from New York, which is good.

One thing which Bob Wallace, from California, says, that interests me, is that many Americans are put off coming to England, because they think that they will be taking food from us which we need. I of course explain that the proportion used in hotels is so small that our rations would remain the same. Also, the Americans are very fond of fish, and think it's a great delicacy. They call it seafood, so why not a poster; 'Seafood for lunch and breakfast in that Isle set in the Silver Sea, England'!

Bob says that we never publicise our beautiful villages, churches, cathedrals, old inns, and matchless countryside. For instance, he thought it would have been great to have stayed at The Bull in Rochester, with its Pickwickian associations, obviously these sorts of things should be publicised to high heaven to attract tourists, likewise things such as Knole and Polesden Lacey. Incidentally, Bob is a student of art and architecture, so would know if much were written in America about our beauties. I shall do propaganda for Somerset, Kent, and Exmoor. It is very strange but in some ways the Americans are more puritanically minded than in England.

At International House, no contact between the sexes is allowed in their bedrooms. Men can never visit the girls' side of the House or vice versa, at either day or night. There is a middle door or partition, which if opened starts bells ringing all over the House, so that is that! When International House was built, Mrs Rockefeller had great difficulty in persuading people to follow her plan of having both men and women in the same house. I think people find themselves minus their rooms very quickly if they are either drunk or causing scandal.

Yesterday at International House, the British Empire group, consisting of Great Britain, Australia, and New Zealand, spent most of the day rehearsing our sketch for the Hallowe'en festival this coming Saturday. We are finding Hallowe'en none too easy to arrange, as the script is causing a good deal of argument. We have spent most of the day on it, much to my annoyance. I think it will be all right in the end, but there is a good deal to be settled and too many people trying to produce and unite. I really wish the English had standard turns to do at International Shows. Had I thought of it in time, I think we might have had a mock trial, always amusing, and not needing too much preparation.

Maeve McPeek, who is a graduate in English Literature, and now works in the registrar's department at the University of Connecticut, is in New York this weekend and is coming to Hallowe'en. I thought I had best return their hospitality and this is a golden opportunity. She will stay at a hotel.

Things are now in that sort of routine which varies a bit from day to day. I went to the first of the graduate seminars for Christians on Wednesday, which caused me to open my mouth! On Saturday I had a few people to my room in the evening for which I bought wine and had cheese biscuits. It was quite enjoyable, except that I had decorated the room with drying socks! I am trying to get some small reproduction pictures for the walls. I have had a photostat copy made of that Bach Cantata no 53 Schlager doch *Sweet is Youthful Death*, which was being played and I was listening to when Phyllis died *(John's sister – SMP)*. It is not printed, as the only publishers are German, and they are quite defunct.

I have received via Mrs Charles Hemming on Fifth Avenue, an invitation to talk about Marshall Aid to the Schenectady League of Women Voters on Nov 10th together with Otto Borch, a Dane who is also a Rotary fellow here at International House. He is rather older and not quite so 'mixing up' with the life here, but is very nice and most interesting. *(Otto subsequently became Danish Ambassador to the UN, Washington and Stockholm – SMP)*

Election Day is a public holiday. In the morning, we shall be in New York, and then in the afternoon I hope to go with 200 other people from International House to a party at the residence of a Mr and Mrs Dodge up the Hudson River, who are wealthy, I am told. A person sitting here with me said that I should write 'filthy rich'. How convenient the 'filthy rich' are at times! In the evening we will go to join the celebrating crowds in Times Square and there wait until the results are known. Truman thinks he will be returned, but Dewey does too, so we don't know.

The Roosevelt Hopkins book is just published here. It is very well reviewed by Professor Commager in the New York Times today, but it is $6, so I shall probably only borrow it from the library. We all continue to have considerable fun with my comments on America, which I make purposely naïve, but the television reply about getting in here easily is still the classical. There are really an extraordinarily nice lot of people here, and I am sure it is making my time in New York much more enjoyable and more profitable, and it will be lovely when American friends, as well as those from New Zealand and Australia etc, decide to visit the great land of their fathers and I can meet them there.

In addition, there are several girls who are in the same set: Marcia from New Orleans, a music student; several Canadian and Californian girls; and a magnificent benefaction of New Zealand to mankind named Beryl Prendergast, who is most dashing in every respect, and who is a delight and joy in a very harmless way! Her father owns racehorses. There are such a lot of good people here that it's hard to list them all, and although I remember faces well and where people come from, names do not always stick.

Cunard was booked up long ago, contrary to what was said in London. I have been to US Lines and they will have something, but I may ask Daddy to see his Cunard masonic friend; there must be some use for it.

John Prior and Beryl Prendergast outside International House. Photo: John Prior

15. GIVE 'EM HELL

500 RIVERSIDE DRIVE
NEW YORK 27, N.Y.

1st November 1948

Last Thursday night I had quite an experience, going to the Democratic Rally at Madison Square Gardens with Bob Andress, from Alabama, and Bill Taylor, from Australia. It is a huge, covered arena, having I think 16,000 or more people there that night, and brilliantly lit. It was all most impressive.

We all thought that we should like to hear him "give 'em hell," and utter the well-known phrases of vigorous denunciation. The rally, which was the climax of Truman's New York visit, was extraordinarily interesting, and we really got quite excited.

From 8 p.m. onwards, for the first two-and-a-half hours, musical items alternated with the lesser speakers, each one being introduced by a noisy interlude from the band. Among the speakers were Herbert Lehman, ex-Governor of New York and UNRRA administrator, and Harold Ickes, ex-secretary of the interior. He bitterly ridiculed Mr Thomas 'elusive' Dewey so harshly that one wondered where he'd leave off! In a delightful speech, he spouted that he understood Mr Dewey was willing now to say that you couldn't tell what the future would bring until it came, and he was soon hoping that he would admit that the past was the past!!

The chief line against Dewey has been his supercilious refusal to do much more than say he wanted unity. Amazingly, within a few hours, we shall know the outcome of this.

To return to Madison Square Garden, at 10.25 p.m. amidst terrific blasts from the band, and the whole audience rising and yelling itself hoarse, in walked Mr Truman, followed by his wife and daughter, Margaret. I had previously seen Mr Truman driving through the streets in an open car, preceded by 101 motorcycles with sirens blowing, and he looks just like his photographs. He is medium height and build, with a cheery smile, and appears friendly. He made quite a good speech, telling a heckler, probably inspired, that he was going to "give 'em hell." The theme of his speech was that Governor Dewey could follow the President to all the tours, but he could not follow him in advocating the particular things which the President advocated in the towns he visited. It was quite skilfully done, although his speaking tone is most uninteresting.

He spoke for half an hour, then after he had finished, Miss Tallulah Bankshead, a famous actress who is the daughter of a southern Democrat speaker of the House of Representatives, came on and thanked him in a nice little speech, and kissed him!

Saturday was of course the great day of the International House Hallowe'en festival. Maeve McPeek stayed in New York for the weekend, so she was able to come to it and that was a good way of returning her hospitality. The whole House was a teeming throng of enthusiastic people milling around to see the various shows, and eating and drinking at the Syrian coffee lounge, the Danish beer garden and other places. Right up until the last moment, it seemed as if the British show would be a failure, as we could not agree on how the story should be done at all. In the end it was most successful, and we were exceedingly popular, many people being nice enough to say that they thought it was the best of the lot!

It was a melodrama in which a cockney charlady spoke the prologue as we walked across the stage, followed by a stage turn, a dance, Noel Coward's Nautical Extravaganza, and finally a quarrel in which a girl dancer stormed off. The stage manager marched on and asked the charlady if she knew anyone to take her place. She suggested her daughter, Felicity, but Felicity's demonstration of prowess was interrupted by my arrival as Lord Foppington, her suitor.

I asked her to marry me and gave her a jewel, which was promptly stolen! Sherlock Holmes and Dr Watson came to investigate, but secretly they were really criminals and, finding the jewel in the charlady's baby's pram, they tried to make off with both it and Felicity. I stopped them by shooting them, I declared that virtue was triumphant, then the stage manager announced, "on with the show". A hilarious male ballet followed, and then we took our bows in the finale.

I think from literally hundreds of congratulations that I did very well. I certainly looked all right, my black trousers, white shirt, black bow tie and black cloak lined with scarlet, with wide lapels and collar showing and a wide gold chain and diamond ornament across the front. I carried a stick and wore a top hat.

The whole of the festival was a rip-roaring success, with the entire house alive with colourful stalls, dances, national food and drink bars, and hundreds of enthusiastic people milling around all the time; it was quite wonderful. And as we ourselves toured we advertised for our various shows by our costumes. I was careful to look elegant the whole time, until I had a candied apple of enormous size covered with sticky sweet, solidified syrup and coconut. The festival lasted from 8.30 p.m. to 2 a.m., so was quite an affair altogether. Hallowe'en here is a great occasion, and children go around begging and dressed up, as they do in England at Guy Fawkes.

Dining at International House is expensive on Sunday nights being all *à la carte*. So last night four of us, Jacques and Eleanor from Canada, and Helen Carr from Australia, went down to 8th Street in Greenwich Village to dinner. It makes a nice change, and for just a little more in the right places one can get a marvellous meal. We drove back by bus, and the illuminated fashion and luxury shop window displays in 5th Avenue were unbelievably gorgeous in every way. We saw lovely short dresses in huge picture frame settings, black dresses against red damask backcloths, and marvellous silver ware.

On Friday, I heard Mr Wallace speak at Columbia University. He comes to a meeting rather heralded as a saviour, but he spoke quite well on 'Academic Freedom'. Although I think he is sincere, he does keep some queer company, and one feels that he could not be voted for. If I were an American student I might feel differently.

One very funny incident in Professor Lynd's lecture last week, was that in discussing 'social prestige', he said that in England alone of all countries, it was measured by the sounds emitted by the mouth when talking, and immediately imitated the accents, 'Oxford' and 'Cockney'. He elaborated the theme and then I wanted to ask a question, so seeing the opportunity for some fun, I did so by saying that I hardly dared open my mouth after what he had said. There was a terrific laugh and he said he became aware of my presence as he was speaking, and hoped I would ask the question. After a riotous few moments, we settled down to the business in hand once again.

Now we are getting ready for election day tomorrow, which is of course a holiday. In the afternoon we go to the Dodge's party, and in the evening, we are having an election party here, and I am making a mock election speech. I shall imitate either Winston Churchill or Laski. I shall probably launder if I get up in time.

The weather here is still marvellous, sunny, and fresh although quite cold at nights.

John Prior as "Lord Foppington" in the International House Hallowe'en Festival, with Maeve McPeek. Photo: John Prior

16. THE TRUMAN MIRACLE

500 RIVERSIDE DRIVE
NEW YORK 27, N.Y.

November 3rd, 1948 4.30 p.m.

I cannot conceive living through a more extraordinary 24 hours than this past day has been. The result is just startling. President Truman was the only person who thought he would be elected. Every Gallup poll; every political commentator of every political party, thought the fight was lost before it was begun. Yet here Harry is in the White House for four years, having swept himself in, given himself resounding victories in both Houses of Congress, and captured many state governorships. It has all been incredibly exciting, and I was just as excited as any American (I should vote for Truman not Wallace).

The Truman miracle is, of course, the main topic of conversation here, and I will tell you of election day. At 8 a.m. I went to Holy Communion, it being All Souls day. Then I came back for breakfast, read, and wrote, most of the morning. At 2.30 p.m., I left by car with several others for Riversdale, just beyond Manhattan, to Mr and Mrs Dodge's residence, where we had a marvellous time. Mr Dodge is a banker, and his house overlooks the Hudson River. It has beautiful grounds, and his many trees were stunning with autumn leaves. We walked around all over the estate, racing up the hills, picking up and eating apples as we went. They have six gardeners, and the head gardener showed a few of us over the greenhouses.

We then went into Mr Dodge's Victorian house, all 200 of us, for refreshments. It was very cosy and comfortable and informal. We just sat and sprawled where we liked and had tons of hamburgers, sandwiches, ice-cream, and cakes, it was not uncomfortably crowded, and we passed from room to room, sampling the different things that there were going. Chocolate in one; tea in another; coffee in another, so many that we were quite full. All the time we were there, a blind man played a Hammond organ in the hall.

Mr and Mrs Dodge were both charming and gave the girls bunches of flowers, and the men buttonholes from their garden. The house was very nicely furnished, with some attractive pictures including ones of Ely Cathedral and the West Door of Rochester Cathedral.

Then we returned to International House where after an hour's reading, I had supper and went to the election night dance there. The results started coming in at 9 p.m., and as we heard them at International House it seemed incredible that our ears were hearing right, that Truman was ahead! Naturally, we just thought it was city votes later to be offset by the Republican votes.

Leaving International House at 11 p.m., we went to Times Square to see the results on the Times building, but it was rather dull and cold, without the usual election night crowds. The announcement circuit around Times Building flashed that the crowd was small and quiet, so we struck up *Rule Britannia!* and we were moved on by the cops!

We returned to International House by 1 a.m., and several of us went to Bob Wallace's room to start listening in to the radio, fortified by sherry, and becoming increasingly enthralled by what was going on. As the hours rushed by, the voting became closer, until it seemed that neither party would have the requisite 266 votes in the electoral college, and that the election would pass to the House of Representatives, where the Dixiecrats might have held the balance.

Then things slowed up; no returns came in, so we listened – would Ohio be for Truman, had Wallace or the Dixiecrats lost him the election, what about Illinois and California? With over 90% of the vote counted, the Democratic majority in Ohio was minute – it wavered – would it go Republican?

We stayed up all night without blinking an eyelid, and descended for breakfast at 8.15 a.m. when there was a lull in the returns, the Senate and House already being Democratic. The voting tensely shifted from side to side and it seemed even around 10 a.m. that Dewey could conceivably win, though everything else was against him. Then, quite suddenly, California went for Truman, just as Ohio was decided, at 11.14 a.m. the Democrats claimed victory, and at 11.16 a.m. Dewey conceded the election.

The radio had all the phases of the election marvellously covered, and the reports from the various states were interspersed by commentaries, all of course nearly speechless with surprise and radio blushes at the fact their forecasts were without exception incorrect. There were full results from all states of the Union with comments by Elmer Davis, Dr Gallup, Elmo Roper, Walter Winchell, and others continuously, their theme being that it was all most surprising, even irregular.

The newspapers have been great fun to read. The Chicago Tribune boldly announced that Dewey had won, and has therefore become a collector's item. The magazine 'Time' had to be entirely reprinted since it had assumed a Republican victory. The result shows that people want the New Deal to continue despite Mr Dewey's 'me too' protestations. They preferred not to put their trust in those in the Eightieth Congress. The elections have been the main topic of conversation ever since then, which has made things lively for us all the time.

Truman is remarkable; against every recorded prediction; with his party thought to be dying and split in three (with Wallace and Thurmond), with himself following a great man, and his own imperfect record; with sixteen years of one party's rule behind him; with few able lieutenants; against a brilliantly organised campaign; against apathy; this man toured the country stopping at every whistle stop, "giving 'em hell," telling them the facts, announcing his policy, making typical blunders on the way. With 80% of the press against him, with no party funds for frequent broadcasts, without the magnetism of FDR, Truman alone appears to have won the country to his side, triumphing in just that field of personal appeal which was said to be Roosevelt's greatest gift and Truman's greatest lack.

He never doubted the result. He said he saw the people wanted him, and they did; in many states he did better than Roosevelt ever had. He got the housewives' vote because of high prices, the farmers' vote because of his subsidies, the labour vote because he 'says he will deal with the Taft-Hartley act'. Above all, he used the fact of the Eightieth Congress with diabolical skill. This must surely go down in history as the most amazing and successful campaign in this century as well as the most vigorous. It proves too, that by not stating its policy, a party like the Republican clearly stands to lose. That lesson was taught to Mr Churchill in 1945 and to Dewey today. The New York Sun said, "This most amazing political upset of the century completely reverses all forecasts and has stunned political leaders, and of course Truman is now in the White House in his own right and will be able to govern well with this popular mandate."

My own observations:

1) Truman won by a direct, personal, at times racy, appeal to the electors using the Eightieth Congress as main target. He was ultra-positive. Dewey obviously thought it a bore, and just appealed as President-elect for unity, which seemed to deprive people of their right of decision.
2) The Election itself was close, but was a resounding personal triumph for Truman, mainly because of the odds. Congress was won more surprisingly, being now peopled by Liberal Democrats or Republicans, some of whom are trying to oust their old guard.
3) It is a confirmation that the people want the security and benefits of the New Deal, and want the country to be progressive in policy, moving left-centre all the time. Businessmen might not agree with this. The Democrats believe, of course, in free enterprise, but demand that it gives social justice, which is opposed by the Right here as in Great Britain. The same with the Taft-Hartley Act compared with the 1927 Trade Union Act; the Taft-Hartley will be repealed or drastically revised. So, I think it is a

moderately progressive, but not a socialist government, partly put in power by organised labour.

4) The polls were accurately taken, but there were 15% 'don't knows'. In previous elections these had been equally split Democratic / Republican. This year, however, the background was 75% Democratic. But no account was taken of that. If they had been considered, and 12% given to Truman, that would have put him in the lead in the polls. In fact, nearly all the 15% voted Republican, so the data was correct, but the interpretation wrong.

5) It cannot be too strongly emphasised how amazing the result is, nor how greatly it was due to the personal success of the Truman family, Bess and Margaret, as well as Harry. It was a fine demonstration to everyone that democracy is alive, fighting, and a real choice by the people. Truman was completely confident, and knew when the results would be out. He slept all night, and got up when he knew things would be turning.

6) It showed that the New Deal of Roosevelt is a force, even without its chief showman and founder, for whom I gain an increasing, if more knowledgeable, admiration.

7) Although it was a resounding personal triumph for Truman, the main point is not the size of his majority, which is small, but the fact that it was against all expectation. His campaigning, all his own work, evidently woke people up, as he stormed over his 22,000 miles of the USA.

Dewey has now admitted his overconfidence, and that people did not like his attitude of 'it's all a terrible bore because I'm already in'.

I am more than ever glad that I stayed up all night and did not go to bed, because it was all so very interesting, and I shall not probably have the opportunity again ever to be present at such a momentous occasion. But the consequence was I slept from 6.30 p.m. until 8.30 a.m., only awaking twice, and completely missing my Christian graduate seminar.

17. A FOREIGN AFFAIR

500 RIVERSIDE DRIVE
NEW YORK 27, N.Y.

9th November 1948

Having recovered from the election, I worked Thursday, Friday, and Saturday morning, spending the afternoon at a meeting at the Waldorf Astoria. That evening I went to see *A Foreign Affair* with Marlene Dietrich, which did not show GIs in too favourable a light, although the Americans who accompanied me seemed to think it very authentic.

On Sunday I went to church in the morning, at The Little Church around the Corner, with Mr and Mrs Diehl, and then on to the Bilbania restaurant by myself for lunch.

In the afternoon, I read the New York Times, and then I went with several others at 5 p.m. to the Ministry of Music at Riverside Church, where they performed part one of *Elijah*, which was excellent, and will be followed by parts two and three on succeeding Sundays. Then we returned to the House for the Sunday night supper, a monthly event at which food and a musical recital is followed by a distinguished person giving a talk in the auditorium. The House originally grew around this institution. Several of us who are British sat with Mr Mott to meet the speaker, Mr Robb MacLachlan, assistant editor of the Economist here on a lecture tour. He spoke on western union, the Commonwealth, and Great Britain.

I sat next to him, and therefore had an interesting conversation. Miss Hayes of the British Information Services was on the other side of me.

After that, there were elections to the student council, which meets next Sunday evening. The British elected me, which was a very great honour, and which excites me somewhat. They are having a buffet supper that night. I hope I shall be successful; I usually am on that sort of thing. I am really rather excited about being in the council, which is an advisory body to Mr Mott, and the experience may be useful in a matter that is increasingly interesting me: the International Language club at Croydon, which is the London equivalent of International House, so far as there is one.

Tomorrow I shall prepare for my talk at Schenectady on 'Britain today and the Marshall Plan and the UN', and I shall make it quite simple. At any rate, the fare is paid, so it will be a nice jaunt.

I have read or looked at most of the Roosevelt literature so far published, good and bad. For my own part I am still a great admirer of his, both for what he did for Americans during the depression and for his social and political ideas in peace and war. But the fact remains that there is a definite hatred of that man and all his works in most business and many professional circles. In England I do not think that would have happened, he being a liberal, left wing when necessary. Some thought he wanted power alone, and was willing to become a dictator to be it. But I admire him more and more.

18. A FUTURE KING

500 RIVERSIDE DRIVE
NEW YORK 27, N.Y.

15th November 1948

It's a prince! Everyone here is quite thrilled! *(birth of Prince Charles – SMP)* We heard at about 6 o'clock in the evening.

    The same evening, there was the first meeting of the student council, which will I think be quite an important body and it is marvellous for me to be involved with it from every point of view. Mr Mott seems to think that we are a genuinely nice group of people this year. At the meeting, us five British people received special congratulations on the royal birth which was rather nice.

    After the meeting, we celebrated the birth by having beers early in the evening, a Chinese meal, and singing *God Save the King* many times at a bar without provoking a revolution! A bar is the US equivalent of a pub, though more like a milk bar open all night selling beer. The singing went on until 11.15 p.m. in the lobby with an enthusiastic group; at midnight we left for a neighbouring bar, where we drank four glasses of beer and staying singing patriotic songs until 2 a.m.

Later, we descended to singing those very French songs, which leave nothing to the imagination and which Prince Philip, as a naval type, might know, though his wife probably would not. But it was all most enjoyable and everyone in the House seemed to think it their duty to shower congratulations upon me, from Mr Mott downwards.

I was able to celebrate rather better than most people in England, for whom as the New York times says, the announcement came after closing time. It is the main news in all the papers today, with leading articles as well.

My earlier engagements for the week went off very well indeed. On Tuesday there was a pleasant hour's candlelight musicale in the Home Room, given by a Canadian tenor who lives here, and is about to tour the States. Otto Borch and I travelled quite safely to Schenectady, and we spoke to the League of Women Voters, each for about thirty minutes on our respective countries. I began by reminding them that as I had no good old days to look back to, I naturally looked forward. It is surprising how much we are completely children of the war and its aftermath, having been born when we were.

I then spoke mainly on the usual post-war difficulties, and the policies of the government in attempting to deal with them, ending up with a few words on Marshall Aid and international affairs which they particularly requested. Afterwards a few questions were asked, and everyone seemed most enthusiastic about the talk and me personally, at any rate I am quite sure that it was rightly to be classed as successful in every respect, and I really quite enjoyed it.

The only annoying thing was that I had to miss a supper for the student council because of it. I did not of course know I should be on the council when I accepted the invitation to Schenectady, but I was sorry to miss it. I have also said I am not going to the play readings any more, as I find that they rather tie me down.

On Friday I went to an experimental school in 110th Street, to talk to boys and girls of sixteen to seventeen years old about education in England. The invitation to do this came from a pupil teacher there, who also lives at International House. She thought I would be able to interest them, so I talked there for forty-five minutes on the framework, administration, finance, curriculum, and general school life in education in England.

They seemed most interested, and it was another good experience. I was surprised how much I knew about education, as I have only really followed developments relatively casually in the press, and never spoken on it before.

Saturday was spent getting money from the bank in the morning, and visiting friends of Bob Wallace at Columbia University College. After lunch we went to the Frick Collection, a museum rather like London's Wallace Collection, and the Metropolitan Museum of Art. This was followed by going to a German *Konditorei* for coffee, and the most delicious cakes you ever saw, real cream jam puffs and something called *Linzertorte*. These foreign restaurants are one of the major joys of New York. The previous evening a whole contingent of us had visited Joe King's Rathskeller, a famous German-American student restaurant where we had a magnificent time. It is one of the famed sights of New York and something not to be missed.

In the evening, there was a dinner of the International House Alumni Association, to which the student council was invited. The dinner was delicious, but the speakers were not marvellous apart from David Rockefeller who was quite good. He is short and stocky. That was followed by a dance. I am amazed at my new-found inventiveness on the dance floor. Although American steps are different from ours, and they do a lot more rhumbas, sambas and tangos, I just dance everything and find that I can invent rhythmic enough steps to please my partner, which is surprising, as I could never count three for a waltz, let alone 'beat the daddy' eight to the bar. It is quite fun which is the main thing.

One thing I notice is that at International House, a far greater proportion of people go to church than I would have expected. On Sunday I attended Holy Communion at 9 a.m., where they provide a complimentary breakfast, and then I went on to church at Union Theological College, with a brilliant sermon by the Professor of Homiletics (look that one up!).

In the afternoon, I went with Bob Wallace and Curtis Green in Kay Barber's car, out to Fort Lyon Park, which is on the high land in Manhattan and is perfectly delightful, overlooking the Palisades and the Hudson River. The weather is still fine and warm which tempted us to go, and we must have been there for two hours walking and talking.

There is also a museum-like collection of odd arches and statues of great worth, culled from medieval France and Europe called The Cloisters.

Future plans include a visit to the theatre to see *Life with Mother* this Thursday, a free concert at the Carnegie Hall on Sunday Night, and a formal dance this Saturday, which will apparently not need tails. On Monday the student council meets again, and on Tuesday the men's class of Riverside Church have invited some of us to go and dine with them, which is free, and therefore good!

Thursday week is an American harvest feast called Thanksgiving, and second only to Christmas as a family festival. I shall be spending it in Boston as the guest of Maeve's Aunt Lydia who has invited me to go there with Maeve's family. I shall be leaving on Wednesday for Connecticut, where I shall stay at Maeve's for a night, and then we go on to Boston for Thursday to her aunt's, staying there a day or two to see Harvard, Boston, Quincy and Concord if possible, returning to New York on Sunday. I am lucky to get such an invitation and it is just what I hoped for as most people seem to be away for Thanksgiving. I think I shall stay at the House for Christmas; it is supposed to be great fun.

The fact about meeting American students at International House is an oblique reference to what is I think probably the major criticism of the International Language Centre in Croydon, that there the foreign students do not live with and intimately know the native English students. Everything at International House will provide me with anecdotes for a lifetime! I think it would be good for the Rotarians to know just that about life here.

19. IT'S LIKE EATING FIRE

500 RIVERSIDE DRIVE
NEW YORK 27. N.Y.

22nd November 1948

I am not having a big spending splash now, but will see how many dollars I have left at coming home time. There is such a lot of interest, value, and enjoyment to be seen here, that I do want to take full advantage of it. There is probably an American phrase or two in my vocabulary by now but not too much.

I prophesy the royal baby will be named George Philip Andrew. Everyone is just thrilled about it, and advertisers are making free use of the theme. On Saturday I went to a great service of thanksgiving for the birth in the Cathedral. It was marvellous, 2000 people there, and the playing of the organ really was jubilant, yet in a dignified slow four-time number of great beauty, a little like Holst's *Turn Back O Man*.

On Saturday night there was a formal dance here. It was exceptionally good and there was no need of evening dress for men. Previously I had been to church at the Little Church around the Corner with Mr and Mrs Diehl, the Rotarian who is overlooking me. I went to lunch with them at an Italian Restaurant which was good. We had fine wine and a marvellous dessert; whipped up egg and sherry (two parts sherry to one egg I should think!) served piping hot, and with sherry the predominant part, my word, it was a little like eating fire!

I afterwards brought them to International House to see the place and they liked it very much. Mr Diehl is seventy-five and has a successful business. He has three sons by his first wife, who died many years ago. He and his second wife, who is around forty, are staunch Democrats, he had known Franklin Delano Roosevelt well since 1910 in New York Democratic politics, and is a passionate admirer of his. He says he is practically the only Rotarian in New York who is a Democrat.

This past week has been quite jolly. On Tuesday I was given a ticket which somebody didn't want at the last moment, for an amusing comedy called *Born Yesterday*, which featured one very funny woman who spoke in a kind of, 'I'm just a woman that can't say no', voice, all the time.

Then on Thursday a whole party of us from International House went to see *Life with Mother* which is a most amusing domestic comedy. Following that we went to the Kleine Konditorei for coffee and cakes.

Last night we had free tickets to a piano concert at Carnegie Hall by Anatole Kirair, which was excellent. He played Bach's *Busoni–Chaconne*, a Sonata (K533) by Mozart, *Wanderer Fantasia* by Schubert, *Fimerailles* by Lizst, a Chopin group, a new piece, and the *Danza Russe* by Stravinsky, plus five encores which were most generous. The hall was not full.

At the student council meeting here last night I was elected secretary of it, which pleases me. It so happens that the Chairman and Vice-Chairman are Canadian and Indian respectively, so it is a Commonwealth affair. Mr Mott thinks that is remarkable, and an accidental tribute to the high prestige which we have. I wrote some minutes for the meeting, which Mr Mott thought acceptable.

I think I will be going on a five-day Rotary speaking tour in Pennsylvania from December 27th– 31st in publicity for the scholarships. There may be a little recompense for it. Otto Borch was asked to do it, but he couldn't. I have had no correspondence with the district governor of Rotary district 177-B there yet, except for having typed him a lengthy letter of introduction for myself, so will wait to see what transpires.

20. A BOSTON TEA PARTY

500 RIVERSIDE DRIVE
NEW YORK 27, N.Y.

1st December 1948

This afternoon I have my talk on, 'Comparative attitudes of the State to Railways in England and the States', for Professor Goodrich's class. It was an interim report on the work that I am doing in this field, and was therefore delivered from notes. The class lasts two hours, and I spoke for one-and-a-half hours of that time altogether. As the class has one professor and two lecturers studying for PhDs among its six members, I was very pleased that I made a good impression and had some fruitful ideas. I was a bit nervous about it before.

The student council is now having its various committees. I do not think there will be a very great deal of work for me, but I am so pleased to be on the council and I like a lot of the other people who are on it.

This evening we had a most interesting talk at the House on, 'The Part of the Myth in Modern Literature, Drama and Psychology', by a professor of Latin and Greek at Columbia University, who teaches Comparative Literature. I asked a question about T S Eliot's *The Family Reunion*, and he said he did not understand it.

It uses the Orestes legend, of course, and I explained the Christian conversion theory for Harry, with Martin Buber's 'I-Thou relationships' and Eumenides as 'The Hound of Heaven', which he had not heard, and he seemed most impressed.

I must now describe my trip to Boston, which is called, 'The Hub of the Universe', and is very much the capital of New England. It is also the city which is most English in customs and looks of any in the USA. We went on a very pretty drive from Maeve's house in mid-Connecticut to Boston on Thanksgiving morning. There is not the variety of Old England in New England, but the landscape is certainly similar.

We arrived for dinner at 12.30 in the afternoon. Maeve's aunt and uncle are both interesting psychiatrists. They live close to Longfellow's House in Cambridge, and about three miles from Harvard. Their house is square and colonial in style, similar to Georgian architecture in England.

For dinner we had sherry to drink; roast turkey, stuffing, cranberry jelly, apple candied sweet potatoes, broccoli au gratin, bananas baked in orange and lemon juice, and gravy. It was a traditional New England thanksgiving meal, though I prefer brussels sprouts and potatoes and bread sauce, which is unknown here. I think here you cannot appreciate the turkey for all the other exotic tastes. You also nibble salad all the time. This was all followed by lemon cream tart and mince tart, more accurately called spice tart. All American tarts, particularly apple, are too heavily seasoned. We had coffee and dessert in their drawing room. In the afternoon we went out by car to Quincy, to see the homes of the Adams family who were people of great importance in American culture and history. In the evening, after cold turkey, we once again settled down to read and talk. It was most convivial.

Friday was entirely given up to seeing the sights of Boston. We saw: Faneuil hall; Old North Church; Paul Revere's House; the Old State House; the site of the Boston Massacre; the location of the Boston Tea Party; the Kings Chapel; St Peters Church; the State House; Louisburg Square; Charles Street; the Common; Trinity Church and the Public Library. Then we had lunch at Durgin Park where I was served a lovely and delectable steak. It was expensive, but I do like one occasionally. This is the first I have bought for myself, and probably the last.

Everything in Boston is certainly most interesting, particularly as we saw the places which were the scenes of the great events which resulted in the severance of the American Colonies from the British Empire.

Much of the architecture could be English, and some of the cultured Bostonians speak with very English diction. In the morning, we went to the main buildings of Harvard University, which are extremely attractive, all red brick and white paint. The Library has a magnificent collection of rare books, all out on exhibition.

In the evening all of us went to see *The Three Musketeers*, which was quite a good film in most ways. On Saturday we continued to see sights, and then I left on the 1 o'clock bus for New York. The bus is certainly cheaper than the train, but I can read better on the train, so I doubt if I shall use buses often. I came back on Saturday; it seemed easier than breaking the journey in Connecticut. It was a delightful weekend, and it was kind of them to invite me.

Back in New York on Sunday, I slept late and therefore went to the cathedral for communion at 11.00 a.m. It began by litany in procession taking twenty minutes, which was the expurgated American edition, and then followed a long sermon partly on the subject of death. The offertory anthem was *And the Glory of the Lord*, from *Messiah*. In the afternoon I went with Bob Andress, from Alabama and Bob Wallace, from California, to a violin and harpsichord concert at the Frick Collection, which was free and therefore in all ways good.

After tea at the House, I went out with Bob Wallace and his aunt from Utah, and her cousin living in New York, to dinner at a nice Chinese Restaurant quite close to here. Each order with a Chinese dinner comes in a large vegetable dish, so everyone orders differently and then there is a fine choice for all. The food is delicious; bamboo shoots; mushrooms; chicken; veal in batter with sauce; shrimp cooked in egg; beef and pepper etc. Really there is so much that it is difficult to know where to put it all safely. Bob's aunt is a lovely lady, and she has invited me to go and stay with her at Logan, which is 80 miles north of Salt Lake City, if I can possibly manage it on my travels.

Bob Wallace and I have a fine scheme for next semester. He suggests that we share one of the double rooms here, as we keep the same hours, have similar interests, and appreciate each other's company muchly. We get on so well together and we think it will be a fine experience.

The room is $2.25 a week cheaper for me than I am now paying, which is pure gain, and I shall like the experience of sharing a room, although of course mainly because he is such a nice person. The room is on the ninth floor with a fine view, judging from its position, although I have not been in it. He is coming to England next summer he hopes, so we shall be entertaining him no doubt. Incidentally, many from the House are coming to England at some point, and I shall have great fun entertaining and showing them things, so far as this allows.

At Christmas I shall probably be staying here at the House. The Americans do not keep Boxing Day as a holiday.

I am now fixed with Walter E Miller, district Governor of Rotary 177B district, to do the four-day speaking trip to mid-Pennsylvania, from December 27th to 30th, where I am to address noon and night meetings of 30 minutes each at eight places on the subject of 'Opportunities of a Rotary Fellow', to encourage interest and support in the aims of the foundation. There may be some recompense attached so that will be good. I am quite looking forward to it, although it will be fairly hard work. I may then go on for the weekend to Washington and stay with Mrs Horner's brother if it is convenient, and return for term on Tuesday, January 4th. This is purely conjectural; I may return to New York directly from Pennsylvania.

21. TOO MANY CAKES AND BEER

500 RIVERSIDE DRIVE
NEW YORK 27, N.Y.

6th December 1948

Both in work, in which I get a lot done, and play, I seem to be having an incomparable time. I am also getting time to read various books like *The importance of Living* by Lin Yu Tang, which is Chinese and interesting, though not Christian. I am quite convinced by being here at International House that one should live away from home for university if conceivable, and I think that being here will probably make me see things from a more balanced point of view than in London.

On Wednesday morning, I wrote letters, before Professor Commager's class. In the afternoon we had a Graduate Christian Seminar, followed by an Education Committee meeting. Then on Thursday afternoon, I went to the Museum of Modern Art, to see silent films starring Sarah Bernhardt and other famous actresses, which was most interesting. Following that I washed and ironed nine shirts on Friday, and saw Miss Clark at the New York Rotary office for a social chat on Friday afternoon. She is charming, and most interested in what I am doing. She thinks I am spending my time wisely. Rotary seem very keen that we shall lead what kind of lives we want to, and do not want us to be at their beck and call all the time.

However, I shall probably go to the Rotary luncheon the week before Christmas, when classes will be over. Miss Clark is glad that I am going to Pennsylvania, and that Mr Diehl and I get on well together. I think it is well to keep in good contact with her, although the money comes direct from Rotary International to me. I think I shall send Rotary International a copy of my circular letter for them to see what kinds of impressions I give friends; but I shall re-read it first.

On Saturday in the morning, I went to class followed by an amazing afternoon at Union City, New Jersey. I went with Kay Barber and Gerald Weales, who is a friend of Bob Wallace's. We drove in Kay's car to collect a $3 slab cake for a meeting Kay was holding, from a friendly baker there called Mr Jaeger. Whenever they go to get things, he entertains them a little. When we arrived, we did not think he was in his bakery, so we had lunch of steak sandwiches and a bottle of dark German beer at a nearby place. Then went to collect the cake and found Mr Jaeger. He soon took us out, gave us all another lunch and three more beers for a sum total of $12.50, and then before we left, he gave us each a fruit cake normally sold for $1.25, a box of *peffenes*, which are little biscuity buns, and a large chocolate iced cake and two smaller ones for us all to share. I have never known anything like it at all, it was quite phenomenal. He has evidently just taken a fancy to us. German beer does not show much evidence of water and is quite potent, at any rate.... well, nothing happened and we got home safely, soundly, and most respectably, really we did. In the evening, Gerald and I sipped coffee, talked, and ate the cake, which was great. Gerald is nicknamed 'Bogey'.

The big event here this last week has been the mission conducted at the Cathedral by Bryan Green of Holy Trinity Brompton, and now Rector of Birmingham. He presented it on the traditional lines of evangelical missions, with conversions, and the amazing thing is his success in this most sophisticated of cities. I was breakfasting after communion with Dr Pitt, visiting Chaplain to Columbia University and Rector of Grace Church and one of the co-chairmen of the mission and he said they expected to get a few hundred people. Instead, they got nearly 6,000 people each night, and last night, 25 minutes before the service began, the crypt was full and 10,000 people were in the Cathedral to hear him, with many turned away.

It is as amazing an experience as you could wish for, especially as we frequently say the old kinds of evangelism no longer work well. He seemed to be getting hundreds of conversions as he had people standing up in verses of hymns. Not only was his sheer inspiration a joy to hear, but when he had those newly converted stand at the end of the service, or go to the high altar, the response was terrific, quite unlike anything I have ever seen in England, and an amazing tribute to the man. And yet people in England say that he has lost his effectiveness.

Mrs MacDonald, the social secretary here, has just asked me to take part in an invitation from Vassar college at Poughkeepsie. Vassar is the poshest women's college here, and we will spend the weekend there in the homes of students, and then go to a formal dance this Saturday. So that will probably show me a richer side of American life than before. I am having my blue suit cleaned and shall buy a new white shirt and new silk tie. I shall not hire a tuxedo, as that is not necessary, I gather, but I might borrow one from somebody about my size here. It will be quite an experience. What a time I do have!

22. DELIGHTFUL VASSAR COLLEGE GIRLS

500 RIVERSIDE DRIVE
NEW YORK 27, N.Y.

14th December 1948

The Christmas cake and pudding sent from England have arrived in perfect condition, just as if they had been brought from kitchen to dining room. The mince pies were a little broken, so Bob and I ate them last night, and they were delicious. Owing to the various regulations here, I shall have a party in my room to cut the cake and serve sherry for some of the men, as no women can be invited unless we book one of the reception rooms, and then we can't serve wine. Pudding will be accounted for later.

    The weekend at Vassar was really one of the most delightful ones that I have ever spent. Every arrangement which the girls made for us was lovely, and so were the people we stayed with. Vassar is one of the most expensive girls' colleges, and has a lovely campus at Poughkeepsie, New York State. The girls who go there have no worries over money, and whizz around in cars quite nonchalantly. We arrived at 3:30 p.m., and after introductions, we were taken to the houses of the people with whom we were staying the night, who were well-off Poughkeepsie families.

Another Englishman, David Johnson, and I, were staying with the Misses Kinkead, two maiden ladies of English and Scottish and Irish extraction who were keen to have young Englishmen staying with them. They own a large house and farm at Poughkeepsie, high overlooking the Hudson River. We went to their house by car.

When we arrived, they were not in, and we were met at the gate by the gardener, who directed us to our rooms which were in a guest wing they keep for the dates of Vassar girls. We left for dinner at Vassar before they returned, and had a fine time where the Vassar girls entertained us in their halls. The dinner was pork and eclairs. The coffee was served in the luxuriously furnished living room, where my 'date', or Vassar hostess, was resident. She was named Dorothy, an architects' daughter, and quite nice.

After dinner, we went to see their experimental theatre production *The Alcester of Euripides*. It was a good and well produced play which deals in part with the second wife question. After that, we waited for an hour while our partners took off what they were wearing and decked themselves in finery for the dance. We were in suits, and I had bought a pair of black socks, *de rigeur* for that kind of thing here, and a new white shirt, likewise a necessity. The girl who was acting as hostess to me appeared in a black taffeta dress, with a silver stomacher, which was most attractive. Some of the dresses were just marvellous, hooped creations and airy net ones. We understand it is customary to have a new dress for each dance! Dancing went on until 1:00 a.m., and was most enjoyable, the dresses in themselves being a real delight, apart from what was inside them!

We returned to the Kinkead's, who were waiting up for us. They are about 55 apiece, and both tall and stout with resounding voices. They have, I should think, pots of money, and a house full of wonderful things, which I studied as much as I could. They have a dairy farm, and I imagine they rule everything with a rod of iron. They have no maid now, but do their own cooking and usually have a houseful. They seemed really delighted to have us, stayed up talking until 2.15 a.m., and gave us literally pints of milk and iced Madeira cake.

The next morning, we had breakfast at 10:30, following the arrival of Minnesota cousins of theirs. Nothing could be passed across the huge dining table because of its size. It was nearly covered with silver jugs and tankards, and vast quantities of the most magnificent silverware. We had porridge with thick cream from their Jersey cows, which was so filling that I took several hours to recover my equilibrium. We were due back at Vassar at 11.00 a.m., but got there at noon owing to the length of time taken in eating breakfast.

Once back at Vassar, we had a picnic lunch in one of the lounges there, and I could hardly eat a thing because of the breakfast; however I won through in the end.

Just as we were leaving to go to lunch at Vassar, and knowing that David was going to Toronto for Christmas, the Kinkeads asked me if I would like to spend Christmas with them. They said they were sure that I should, and that they would be having some Vassar girls there as well. So, I am coming back to Poughkeepsie on Thursday 23rd December until Sunday 26th December, just before my Pennsylvania tour. Isn't that nice? Of course, I am sorry to be missing Christmas at International House, but this is so marvellous an invitation, and they are such wonderful people. I think that they will have superb food and well served too.

After lunch at Vassar, we looked around a bit and I returned to New York by car in time for Sunday supper, to which we had invited Mr Jaeger from Union City. We sang Beethoven following the meal, and then watched a film on displaced people in Europe. Mr Jaeger took us back to Union City in his Cadillac, where we had some beer, and I had a Yorkshire Buck; rich thick hot cheese with fried bacon and a poached egg on toast. Then before we departed, we had a little glass of Benedictine and Brandy, it is excellent. I had no ill effects on Monday, though Bob felt strange.

Last night we went to the Union Theological College carol service by candlelight, which was standing room only. It was like King's Cambridge but more international in the choice of carols. They had quite elaborate holders on each pew to hold the candles at about eight feet off the ground. I didn't know many of the carols. A Scotch one *What Strangers are Then*, arranged by Richard Powis, is particularly fine.

Tonight, I am writing a report for Rotary International. They have altered the regulations and want one about now. I had intended originally writing after Christmas, as that would have suited me better when I have more news.

Tomorrow, the Graduate Christian Seminar is dealing with the question of the university which should be good. Last night the executive committee of the privy council met, and I typed the minutes this morning. Thursday night is a candlelight service at Columbia University to which I shall go followed by either a Christmas party at Riverside church or by a concert of Bach Christmas music. I shall have to see which I choose.

On Saturday, I hope to be going to hear *Messiah* at Carnegie Hall if Bob can get tickets today. On Sunday, there is Riverside Church Carol service, when they are performing Benjamin Britten's *Ceremony of Carols*, Vaughan Williams' *Christmas Hymn*, and Buxtehude's *Dulci Jubilo*. On Monday, there is a party I may go to and on Tuesday, I am going to one at the English-speaking union. My Christmas will not be a dull one.

Southwood, Poughkeepsie, home of the Misses Kinkead. Photo: *John Prior*

23. CHORUS GIRLS DRESSED UP AS POODLES

500 RIVERSIDE DRIVE
NEW YORK 27, N.Y.

19th December 1948

(The reader should note that this chapter contains expressions which are reflective of the era in which they were written and are now considered offensive - SMP)

We are now in Bob's room at 12.30 a.m., listening to *Messiah* after an hour's play in the snow in the little park in the front of the House, which was really good fun. There are nineteen inches of snow which have fallen today, so we are looking quite Christmassy and I shall have to get some snow boots. The snow is the third heaviest fall in New York's history, 18,000 men are engaged in clearing it, which sounds amazing!

Earlier in the evening, nine of us had assembled to eat the iced cake sent from England, and the tin of ginger biscuits. We had a bottle of Spanish sherry and Californian Muscatel, which were much appreciated. My guests were Bill Taylor from Australia, John Graham from Canada, Bob Andress from Alabama, Bob Wallace from California, Curtis Greer from Georgia, Bogie Weales from Indiana, and Duncan and Nipper from New York, so probably no English cooking has ever been eaten by people of so many different countries.

This being a puritanical country, we cannot invite girls to our rooms, nor serve hard liquor in the public rooms, so I just entertained the men. The pudding sent from England will be eaten at Poughkeepsie; if I must go by sleigh I shall still go. I am sure the trains will be all right.

On Thursday afternoon, the snow had melted. I went to the candlelight carol service at Columbia University with the choir holding candles, and they sung some nice carols that I did not know. The Americans have a hideous tune to O *little town of Bethlehem* which was written by a Boston cleric, one to a melody of Handel, *Joy to the World*, and a Handel tune to *While Shepherds Watched*. In the evening I went to a Christmas party in Riverside church. They have an amazing number of halls, kitchens, bowling alleys, office rooms, and assembly halls, all in the tower or basement.

Saturday was a great day. In the morning I went with some others to Music Hall at Radio City at Rockefeller Centre. The Christmas show was a circus called 'The Rockettes', who are the internationally famous resident troupe of chorus girls. They were all dressed up as poodles. There was a film called *Words and Music*, and the famous nativity scene. For this, Christmas trees are lit at the sides of the stage and around the stairs leading from the side walls, where angels descend to the accompaniment of carols enacting the coming of the shepherds and kings, against a back cloth of a lone star in a swiftly moving cloud. Finally, the stable is shown.

There are beautifully lit Christmas trees everywhere, including in most of the shops, and a huge one in Rockefeller Plaza, which I have not yet seen lit up, but I shall before going to Poughkeepsie.

After that I had lunch at a nice place just off 5th Avenue, of French-fried turkey sandwich and rum raisin spice cake. In the afternoon, I went shopping. I bought another white shirt, four pairs of very strong socks, red and brown ones, that are practically fool proof so far as holes go, and some utensils for eating the Christmas cake. I also bought a catchy little number called *Buttons and Bows*. Then in the evening I went to see a good German film called *Marriage in the Shadows*. The previous days, by contrast, were occupied in writing seventeen letters and doing a report for Rotary International. On Friday evening I played piano for an hour, accompanying carol singing in the lobby, and then showed a Scot around who was staying in the House for a few days.

On Sunday I went to church with the Diehls in the morning, and then they took me back to their house where we had a drink, followed by lunch at Deauville's at Lexington and 74th. We had shrimp cocktail, consommé with dumplings, roast duck, potato and cauliflower, and mince tart. It was delicious. Their house is pretty marvellous, and I think he must be really well off. He has done everything, it seems, and owns an apartment house in the best residential section of New York, where he hopes to move at some time.

The house is entered from street level, and has an entrance hall from which stairs lead to the living room. This is two storeys high, and in one corner an enclosed staircase leads to their bedrooms. When you get to the top of the stairs, you are on a balcony from which the bedroom stairs lead off. These balconies overlooking the room have little iron balustrades, which make a delightful corner to the room. They have a beautiful piano, on which I played Schumann's *Traumerai* at sight and they thought I had a good touch. They have good modern furniture, and really are nice people, so it is always pleasurable to be able to see them.

Then yesterday afternoon I went to the tea here at International House, with Christmas trees and candlelight. In the early evening some of us went over to one of the negro Hudson Methodist churches, and there we had a marvellous service, they did a cantata called *The Stay of Christmas*, by Matthews, and the negro voices were really something to remember. They also sang Stanford's *Magnificat in B♭*, very vigorously, but it sounded effective. The negro voices ringing out through the church are of course famed, and it seemed as if they were ever better in their own setting.

For the future Monday and Tuesday, I shall be working with a party at the English-Speaking Union on Tuesday night. On Wednesday I will prepare the talk for Pennsylvania, then I am to go to the fireside Christmas chat in the House Room and talk about the English Christmas. It occurs to me that I should explain that the next semester does not begin until January 31st; the first three weeks of January being the tail end of the first of the two semesters into which the year is divided.

The Americans make even more of Christmas than we do, with more and more elaborate Christmas trees and candlelight services. All the shops are marvellously decorated, and cafes have meals by candlelight. Lord and Taylor's is all decked in white, and hung from the ceilings are dainty little bulbs in pink, green, yellow, and mauve, all entwined in tinsel strings and arranged in huge groups.

On Thursday I shall go to the Rotary luncheon, and then out to Poughkeepsie, then I return to International House and head straight off on the midnight train to Pennsylvania. I am to give eight talks, and there will be a monetary present of some kind.

I am coming back here for New Year's, as to go to Kay's would probably not be too convenient for her, and I have decided I would rather try Washington outside of the festive season. New Year at the House should be quite good, there is a formal dance, from 10 p.m. to 3 a.m. to see the New Year in, and parties all day New Year's Day, which is made far more of here than in the UK.

24. POUGHKEEPSIE CHRISTMAS

SOUTHWOOD

POUGHKEEPSIE, N. Y.

Southwood
Poughkeepsie NY
Telephone 349

Christmas Day, 1948

Just a quick note on Christmas Day. The Misses Kinkead, and other people here, are giving me the most marvellous time, and I am enjoying every minute of it.

It is now 1.30 p.m. and we do not expect to be having dinner until 3 p.m. We did not arise until 10 a.m. when we heard the king's speech. We went to midnight communion after a marvellous day yesterday. We shall be fourteen people for dinner today, and the English pudding is being cooked under my supervision especially for the occasion. It smells as if it will be particularly good. I have been decorating the house this morning, and putting Christmas cards up on the curtain.

The Misses Kinkead are delightful people, I am playing the piano quite a lot which they seem to appreciate. The food is terrific! Four fried eggs and six rashers of bacon yesterday, plus porridge, cream and a whole grapefruit for breakfast.

More detailed account to follow.

JMP.

25. COCKTAILS WITH THE ROOSEVELTS

27th December 1948

The Christmas party here at International House on Wednesday evening, 21st December, was marvellous. We popped corn over the open fire, and I gave an account of English progress through the Christmas period, largely in terms of food.

I went to Poughkeepsie on Thursday afternoon, after attending the New York Rotary luncheon, and arrived at the Kinkead's at 6:30 p.m. Elise Kinkead's letter to me had warned me that they 'were apt to be a little late', so I should hang around at the station for them. When Jennie Kinkead collected me, she said immediately, "we are apt to be a little late." It just about sums the situation up perfectly; they're always saying it and it hits them off. I was the only person staying at their house, but there were crowds visiting them all along.

On Thursday evening, I was nearly exploded by having to eat mushroom soup, a cut of homebred; killed; and cured pork nearly the size of a hymn book, followed by a rich chocolate pudding and clotted cream; my, what a meal. I played the piano most of the evening, and greatly appreciated the opportunity to do so informally. I am nervous of doing it in front of people.

On Friday morning, we arose late, and had a little breakfast consisting of one whole grapefruit; porridge with very thick cream; four fried eggs; six slices of bacon; and toast and coffee!

The Kinkeads then said that Annie Garrigue, from Vassar College, who lives at Hyde Park, just north of Poughkeepsie, was going to entertain me on Friday, and would call at about 11 a.m. She had driven me around on my first Vassar visit.

Annie arrived, and we played the piano for about an hour and then went out to lunch with her brother Paul, known as 'PG'. I spent the rest of the day with her, and what a day it turned out to be. She took us to Vassar Alumni House, and on to her own house. Her parents have a boarding school for very young children who also happened to be Rockefellers, or Rowntrees, or Roosevelts. They are obviously rich and are extremely nice people with a very stylish house. They have a delightful grand Steinway piano in their beautiful living room.

Annie announced that we were delivering presents, some to Millbrook, twenty miles away, and others to Mrs Eleanor Roosevelt, her son Elliott, and his wife Faye Emerson, who is a famous actress. This of course quite thrilled me, and so off we went. We duly visited Millbrook, had tea there, and noticed all the gaily decorated and lighted houses, with evergreen wreaths at the doors. Americans do decorate far more than the English, and their houses are riots of festive colours against their white wood exteriors.

Having left Millwood, we decided to deliver the Roosevelt presents, and therefore set out for their respective cottages on one huge estate in Hyde Park, away from the President's residence. We managed to reach Mrs Roosevelt's house after being directed by Anna Boettiger, her daughter. We did not see Eleanor and left the present of fruit for her. We then tried to get to Elliott's residence, which President Roosevelt used as his 'Dream House'. On this property the Christmas trees are grown which Elliot sells on New York stalls, for lower prices than the regular merchants, to their terrific chagrin. This 'Val-kill' house is on top of the hill, but we just slid backwards on the icy roads, so we never got there.

We returned to Annie's House, and then the fun really began. We were discussing what to do in the evening, and our only appointment was church with the Kinkeads at 11 p.m. Then Annie said that Elliott Roosevelt and Faye were coming in for cocktails that night, and would I like to stay. I of course said "yes" which quite surprised her, as rich Republican Hyde Parkers refuse to acknowledge the Roosevelts, and usually decline invitations to dinner if any of the hated family are to be there. Socially the Roosevelt family, especially Elliot and Faye, are not acknowledged in Hyde Park by many people. The Kinkeads could not be told that I had met them, as they would have thought it very wrong of the Garrigue's. However, the Garrigue's like Elliot and Faye very much, and they are very friendly with them.

Elliot and Faye are very modern it's true. They are both twice divorced and have previous children. I of course asked to meet them, so after a perfectly delicious meal of lamb chops, ice cream and fudge sauce, Mrs Garrigue rang up Faye, and asked if they were coming. They said, "of course, darling," and that they would be there between 9:30 p.m. and 10 p.m., so naturally we were all highly elated. That time came but no Roosevelts arrived. Just at 10:45 p.m. there was a terrific banging and amidst great cries of affection, Faye entered, followed by Mrs Eleanor Roosevelt and Elliot, so wasn't that absolutely incredibly wonderful? They sat down, and we drank a bottle of champagne specially bottled for President Roosevelt, and listened to Mrs Roosevelt talking, just as I have heard her over the radio.

She is just like her photographs, charming and most attractive. She was in a mauve dress; rust Harris tweed double breasted coat with a fur collar; a huge purple orchid; a black hat over one eye, which I think was the same hat she wore in London for the statue unveiling; brown shoes; and white knitted gloves. It was rather a weird mixture, she had no makeup; curly hair; and salmon pink varnished fingernails. She smiled and seemed so pleased to see everyone and was most jolly, drinking the champagne.

Faye was likewise charming, very much an actress, everyone was "darling," although to sit in a rocking chair with legs crossed and one cocked up is provocative to say the least, especially as I was sitting on an extremely low sofa. She has sure caused a furore by accidentally cutting her wrists with a razor blade.

The papers reported that this was attempted suicide as the result of a family quarrel. She had on a mink coat; a blue and silk taffeta dress; she had short blonde hair, and a pill box over one eye. Elliot is a large man, quite good looking and very charming saying, "Mummy what do you think of that?" Of course, the razor incident was an accident, and they are obviously in love.

They stayed about fifteen minutes, and then rushed off to Hyde Park church, which they always do on Christmas Eve. I think it was just marvellous to meet them and evidently the Garrigues had told Faye on the phone that I was there, and wanted to meet Mrs Roosevelt, so they brought her along, which is really wonderful, was it not?

The Kinkeads think it is an insult to have to meet Elliot and Faye, so I could not breathe a word to them, on Mrs Garrigue's orders, as she is friendly with them. Mrs Garrigue says that the rest of their neighbours take no notice of the Roosevelts, because of their politics, President Roosevelt, and the fact that they all live rather well. However, I was completely charmed by all of them. You may imagine how I jumped for joy and ran up and down in my room at the experience.

We then went to midnight communion, and I inclined to the view that a carol service of thanksgiving or even a non-communicating mass is the proper thing at midnight, with people making communion in the early morning, not directly after hectic decorations, tart making and other Christmas preparations.

On Christmas day, we listened to the king's speech, and then after that at 10:10 a.m. we began to get breakfast, when I managed to have only one half-grapefruit, porridge, two boiled eggs and bread and butter. I then began helping their two maids in the kitchen and put up some Christmas cards. They had not asked their guests to come to dinner before 3 p.m., so we had plenty of time to get ready. By the time people arrived, we had the table all laid for fourteen people; red candles on the tables in countless candlesticks with four candles on branches; a huge centrepiece of evergreen and much silver; and a gold and white dinner service.

Before Christmas dinner, I took a four-mile walk to Poughkeepsie and back to fetch the post, work up an appetite, and get some exercise. Their guests were cousins from across the way, an old, retired clergyman, a crusty genealogist and his sister Cornelia, cousins from New York, and then a family called Newton from Millbrook, who are, I think, very well off, he being a New York lawyer and head of the coal administration during the war. The dinner was tomato soup, followed by the 26-pound turkey, which was delicious. It had various kinds of nut and onion stuffing and cranberry sauce, candied sweet potatoes, broccoli, and probably other things as well.

I had two large helpings, but by incredible skill managed to avoid having a third. That was followed by the Christmas pudding, including the one from England, for which I had made white sauce. Everyone thought how delicious it really was. I think we were all too full for dessert which we did not have formally, but we ate lots of sweets and nuts and figs around. We had sherry with the meal. By that time, as you can imagine, it was getting fairly dark and after a good deal more talking, most of the guests left. Mr Newton and I did the washing up and managed to find where all the china lived, which was a great achievement. When everyone had gone, the Kinkeads and I had some music, and went to bed moderately early.

The next day being Sunday, 'apt to be a little late', we arrived at church at 11:20 a.m., joined the carol service, and heard the sermon. I went to lunch with the Newtons, and had magnificent steak, fried onions and potatoes, followed by apple tart and ice cream, with sherry before lunch. They live out in hunting country, as their daughter Sally, who is at Vassar, likes to hunt. Mr Newton lives in New York during the working week in an eighteen-room penthouse in the Park-Madison district. They have a large living room, with grey walls and pale olive-green curtains and upholstery to match, and the most delightful little dining room.

We stayed there until nearly four, when we went to see a chancel play at the Poughkeepsie church. We were late and told the Kinkeads afterwards, "well we were here on time, but we are apt to be a little late!" After that, we all went back to the Kinkeads for a little light supper of scrambled eggs, assorted cheeses, salad, milk, and coffee.

Mr Newton and I returned to New York, and he was most interested in all that I could tell him about Britain now. He was particularly impressed by my reports of utility clothing. Mr Newton has two younger sons aged fifteen and eleven, and his daughter Sally is very charming. Both her and Mrs Newton sport mink coats.

Now, to come to the events following Christmas. I'm actually writing this from the Penn-Lee hotel in Shamokin, Pennsylvania, after delivering the second of my talks to the Rotary clubs here. I spoke first of my pleasure at being there, then of the history of the Rotary foundation and why it was a good memorial to Paul Harris, and why the fourth aim of Rotary was a difficult one. Then I described the work of the foundation, particularly what the opportunities of the fellows were. I developed the idea that by the foundation, the Rotary International and Rotarians had delegated to specifically chosen people such as myself their concern for international goodwill, in the hope that by their special opportunities, they would be able to think about, and do, good things in their lives.

I followed that by giving a short history of myself, and a description of what I am doing here, together with an account of life at International House. Having completed all that, I then gave a few details of how the scholarships were chosen and administered. I ended with a few resounding impressions of the USA, and some thoughts on what the Labour government is trying to do in England.

I had no set jokes in the talk, but I made various quips that they appreciated, one was that I had discovered that one or two Americans did not think Franklin Delano Roosevelt to be the greatest American yet, so I had them laughing occasionally. And I have a general joke about American words, as I noticed typically American phrases in their bulletins describing the meeting. I would say that as I understood the King's English, and not the president's American, I wasn't certain if I approved of what I was taking part in! I am doing a variant on the same one for all eight talks.

The Pennsylvania countryside is, I think, more like the English countryside than that of New England. The Susquehanna Valley in which these towns are situated is exceptionally beautiful, with quite high hills. Shamokin is an anthracite town.

The district governor, Walter E Miller, seemed overjoyed at me being there, and I may do more talks for him later. He is driving me from place to place. Tonight I am staying at a hotel which Rotary have paid for. I spoke in Milton at lunch having travelled there overnight, and rewritten my talk on the journey, as the first draft did not look right.

Tomorrow we go on to Lock Haven, which is 100 miles from here, and then Mount Carmel. On Wednesday we travel on to Pottsville and Ringtown, then on Thursday we are at Schuylkill and Sunbury. I shall then return to Milton and spend the night with the bank manager I breakfasted with this morning.

Yesterday for the first time ever, I went up in a little Piper aeroplane family cruiser, to get a view from the air. It was quite interesting, and particularly good of the owner of the plane, a Rotarian, to do it. But we only just circled so I hardly know whether I like flying or not.

Annie Garrigue. Photo – John Prior

26. A PRIVATE CHAT WITH ELLIOT ROOSEVELT

500 RIVERSIDE DRIVE
NEW YORK 27, N.Y.

3rd January 1949

I arrived back from Pennsylvania with a gift of $105, plus expenses, and have been rearranging my room and pressing my suit since then. I also sublet my room, #522, through the House over Christmas and received $6.95 in rent. I shall probably buy a typewriter, a Parker GI pen, and a few odd clothes.

The Pennsylvania tour was rather more tiring than I expected, mainly because I was travelling by car all the time. I had no fresh air and was not really able to relax at all. I travelled with Mr Miller, a Rotarian and Chief Governor, in the car all the time. So, it was no picnic, even though I enjoyed it and I do feel that I've been able to discharge a part of my duty effectively. The money is lovely. Mr Miller realises that all is grist to the mill.

I returned to International House in time for the New Year's dance. We had paper streamers and general jollification, whistling and shouting at midnight, followed by supper by candlelight at 12:15 a.m. which was a salad, ice cream and coffee nicely served. It went on until 3 a.m. and I was at the cathedral at 9 a.m. the following morning! New Year's is more celebrated here than in England.

Today, all our southerners and northerners and Canadians have been returning, and there has been a joyful gathering in reunion of the clans, and exchange of Christmas experiences to each other's delight. And now we settled down to work again after only thirteen days off.

I had another marvellous weekend up at Poughkeepsie; or more accurately Hyde Park, staying with the Garrigues. I took an Australian called Bill Taylor from International House with me at their invitation and we had a marvellous time, quite exciting and exhausting. The Garrigues are nice people, and they impressed me very much as being both well-connected, intelligent, and charming.

On Saturday afternoon we just talked, then they had a party in the evening. They had as guests two girlfriends of Annie's, one of whom is at Smith College and one at Vassar; some friends of Annie's brother, Paul, known as PG; a Margo, staying with Annie; a certain Barbara; and also older people including Elliott and Faye Roosevelt. The party was marvellous, cocktails followed by baked ham, scalloped oysters, pies, potatoes, sauces, and ice cream. We all had a fine time, and of course it was most interesting meeting the Roosevelts again. Faye is witty and quite clever, every match of product of stage and screen, but charming and vivacious, and has some very brilliant conversation.

Bill Taylor and I had a long chat with Elliot, in which he expanded his views on Britain's present predicament with considerable force and much interest. He thinks that the Commonwealth is a United Nations and that, if economically it can be further knit together to help itself, it will become the complete illustration.

We think that Elliot so welcomes the chance to talk to people who are not prejudiced against him by the various garish details of his life, which is like Jacob's coat in its colouring. All the Roosevelt children seem to be trying to do something to justify themselves as their father's children but have rather a feeling of inferiority in trying to do it. I think they honestly wish to be useful, but find it a little difficult, and therefore tend to back the most extraordinary schemes.

And of course, the 90% Republican press seizes any chance to hound the Roosevelt name, so they've not much chance. His every action is unfavourably dramatised which is rather bad for them. There has truthfully been much dramatic material, with three wives, various financial irregularities and so on. In all this Elliot is the chief victim, he is quite obviously Eleanor Roosevelt's favourite son. But they are a fiery family. With us I think he probably knew he was being appreciated as the Roosevelt for what he was saying, from people who were outside the orbit of his father's controversial projects. In Hyde Park they have no friends but the Garrigues, which is sad, I think.

At about 10:30 p.m., the Roosevelts having gone, we went out tobogganing down a hill. On each of four times I went down, starting in different directions, my toboggan was attracted towards a tree, and I therefore zoomed off at any possible angle resulting in many bruises in several places, and delighted laughter from the spectators, but I couldn't help it, so what? We young people then had another kind of beer party with the gramophone and singing and retired at 3 a.m.

On Sunday morning, we did not arise until 11:30am as everyone was tired. I had been to church early New Year's Day, as I thought we should be late up and miles from the church. We had a huge ham, bacon and egg breakfast, and followed that by good discussion until 3 p.m., when we left to look over the Hyde Park home of Franklin Delano Roosevelt. This is now open as a museum, it is not the house where the Roosevelts now live. It was around two miles or more away.

We then sat talking until 7 p.m., and I played almost my complete piano repertoire. Bill Taylor, PG, and Annie and Margo Spear thought I played beautifully, and Bill couldn't understand why I hid my talent. I explained my playing was hit or miss but I may gain confidence in playing before people. I carved turkey for dinner last night as Mr Garrigue was out, and they thought I had done well on a ham. We ate great quantities, with all the various trimmings which was delightful. We left for New York after supper, seeing all the Roosevelts at the station, but not to speak to.

I returned from Poughkeepsie last night, and today Bill Taylor and I spent lazily entertaining Annie and Margo here at International House, as they were in New York seeing Margo on a train to Massachusetts and Annie seeing people in New York. Tomorrow back to school, the end of an exciting vacation!

There is one piece of bad news. The Rotary International financial straits with frozen funds are so bad that they will have to pay me the money in London. They say they must take every chance of conserving their dollars and can already scarcely operate because of exchange control. I think I shall still travel to the west, because the Governor is taking a hand in getting me speaking engagements with pay there, likewise around New York.

27. THE FOOLISHNESS OF MAN AND THE WISDOM OF GOD

500 RIVERSIDE DRIVE
NEW YORK 27, N.Y.

10th January 1949

(The reader should note that this chapter contains expressions which are reflective of the era in which they were written and are now considered offensive. SMP)

Last Tuesday, we returned to classes and I have been working hard ever since, although I have had some quite early nights as I had a sore throat and have been more tired than I should have been. The executive committee of the student council met last Thursday, and I successfully dictated the minutes to Mr Mott's secretary the next day.

On Saturday afternoon I saw *The Medium* and *The Telephone*, two American operas, which are rather good. On Sunday morning Reinhold Niebuhr preached, so we all went off to hear him. It was a very fiery sermon on the foolishness of man and the wisdom of God. He is most impressive, but how incredibly restless he is. He draws enormous crowds everywhere he goes, and half the House seemed to be there. It is however a fact that the American people, especially in the country and small towns, are a more going church-going than the English, which may surprise, but it's true.

I read all Sunday afternoon; then heard the first of a series of lectures to be given here on the United States, by Bernard deVoto, a critic. It was followed by supper and then early to bed.

This coming Tuesday, the 'International House Players' are performing two plays, *Hands across the Sea* by Noel Coward and *No Exit*, also known as *Huis Clos*, by Jean Paul Sartre. My friend Beryl Prendergast is in *No Exit*.

So far, I have not bought a typewriter. The new portable ones are $87.00, which is more than I want to pay and then I should not have much left for the odd few items of clothing upon which my heart is set. The best dodge seems to be to get a guaranteed rebuilt model of reliable make, which might also help me get it through the customs.

I have spent $10 on books, $6 for the Roosevelt Hopkins book by Robert E Sherwood, *The White House Papers of Harry L Hopkins*, of which the first part covering up to December 1941 has been published in England. The American version goes right down to Hopkin's death. I have also bought a lovely book of folk songs, carols, negro spirituals, and marching songs which are popular here this year, and it contains a lot of songs that I have become fond of. It is very finely produced, with attractive illustrations, and will be fun for when I return home.

Last night we had another chopstick meal, which was good; and on Saturday evening we said goodbye to two English architect students from Liverpool who have been studying here, so the English contingent at International House is now reduced to four.

Here are some random thoughts on life in New York that do not seem to belong anywhere else. The newspapers from England usually arrive in bundles, about two to three weeks late, but I enjoy having them. Bus fares are eleven cents anywhere in Manhattan, and seven cents on one or two cross town routes. Railway fares are a little more and seem terrific because of the distances involved. I still think our Rolls Royces are more elegant, but the American cars certainly have plenty of room inside, and usually travel at 60 miles per hour on the open roads.

There are plenty of coloured students in colleges here. In the north and west at any rate they are accepted, but maybe they would not be so welcome in all homes here in the east.

28. A RICH WALL STREET LAWYER

500 RIVERSIDE DRIVE
NEW YORK 27. N.Y.

18th January 1949

I am writing this with my new pen, a Parker 51 fountain costing $13.50, blue with all chromium fittings. It is very slick and stylish, and the ink flows marvellously, quite suits my writing, and may help to make it in some way more legible, because I don't think some people find it too easy to read. I also bought a V-necked long sleeve pullover, in Shetland wool natural shade, for $4.95 at a sale. It is beautiful and soft and a real bargain. I have added *The Nature and Destiny* by Reinhold Niebuhr to my book collection.

I shall thus have around $40 of the Pennsylvania Rotary money left. With that I shall get shirts, a corduroy jacket which is a useful and attractive garment, a pair of slacks, a pair of shoes, and an oddment or two, not bad for four days Rotary speaking.

This is what I have done about the typewriter, which pleases me immensely. An exceptionally fine man from the House offered to sell me his for $30, so I bought it. This was more than he could have got commercially for it; and less than I should have had to pay even for a rebuilt one. It is a dear little portable Remington, and in excellent repair. The type is small, but I like it, and that is the main thing.

The keys are adjusted by a lever to sit down when not in use, and thus the whole machine packs into far less space than the more modern portables do. The people to whom I have shown it seemed to think that I have a bargain. I think that it will give me a great deal of use but now I must try to learn touch typing, which must involve similar techniques to playing the piano without looking at the notes.

The past week has been mainly devoted to preparing rather feverishly for exams. I had one in American economic history this morning, which was not too bad, and I shall hope for the best. I also have one in Professor Lynd's course on Thursday. For two other courses I am submitting papers, but Professor Commager's has no exam or paper attached to it. All he expects me to do is to know anything about English life; thought; or letters that he may ask, which is a tall undertaking. The exams here that end all courses are a bit of a nuisance, but this system does at least limit the extent of knowledge required to what has been taught in a particular course.

Then at the end of last week, we registered for the new semester which begins on January 31st. I think this is when Bob and I will be moving to our new room. I am pleased with all the work that I've been doing up until now, and really do think that it is giving maximum value to the idea of the Rotary fellowships.

Last Thursday I had my shopping expedition downtown, and then in this evening I had dinner with an old Mid-Whitgiftian *(John's old school – SMP)* called Norman Topp. He is working in Washington and was in New York for a few days. We passed a pleasant evening having a good French dinner and followed that by long discussions of the school and all its works. Even though he left in 1931, there were a lot of the masters who were common to us both.

Then Friday was a working day, followed by Bob's birthday on Saturday. For this we went with Eleanor Roberts and Kay Barber. Kay is like a mother to us; she is 34 or thereabouts; and a nurse. She warns us of when we ought to wear coats for the cold etc! We had lunch at a French restaurant called The Champlain, having skilfully told Eleanor and Kay that they were paying their way. We had liver pate, followed by London broil of beef, and French seven-layer cake saturated with rum, all for $0.85.

We then went to see an intimate revue called *Heard an Ear*, which was excellent, innocent of all vulgarity, and delightful. One number was called *Neurotic you and Psychopathic me*, another was of a lady cellist singing an old ballad, with explanation preceding, just brilliant. There was also a skit on a 1928 musical *The Gardenia Girl*, which with the dresses of that period was very humorous. After the show we went to the German *Kleine Konditorei* for coffee and cakes.

Then I had an evening's work before an absolutely sumptuous midnight feast in Bob's room. We ate rich fruit cake; fudge; pears; cherry pie; honey bee cake, which is a sort of Madeira bread, fairly moist with cream and sticky nutty top; and sherry and cherry rocher, a kind of French cherry brandy.

On Sunday I went to Holy Communion at 9 a.m., and then to the Harlem church I went to at Christmas. The huge church was packed, and the singing by both choir, and people, was really fine. They sang *Onward Christian Soldiers* in so majestic a fashion that I liked it for once; they made it sound a thousand times better than I could have imagined was at all possible.

Then on Sunday evening, for dinner we went to the Czechoslovak Praja, where for $1.25 we had soup; roast duck, which was otherworldly; peas; dumplings; sliced peaches; bun and coffee. It was delicious in every respect, and a real treat for us all.

On Monday, David Johnson and I met Mr Newton, whom we knew from Poughkeepsie, at his law office at 2, Wall Street, and spent the day with him. He is one of twenty partners in his law firm; they have fifty-two lawyers on the staff and three floors of a skyscraper furnished more like a lush apartment than a lawyer's office. He showed us all around their offices, and then took us to the Federal and State courts, followed by lunch at the Downtown Club, where we had trout. This is one of the most famous of the Wall Street clubs, in fact one of the great places in New York.

Today was the last session of Professor Goodrich's seminar, and he held it in his apartment, and served beer and refreshments afterwards, which was really very nice indeed.

The normal meals at International House are good, but not exciting after an initial surprise at always being able to buy milk, ham sandwiches and salads and that sort of thing, and in bulk I eat less here than in England. For breakfast I rarely have more than milk, grapefruit, and muffin. The costs are reasonable; I allow $2 for food per day, and we only ever eat in the cheaper places in New York as the American good places are prohibitive and just charge for useless service.

29. GONE WITH THE WIND

500 RIVERSIDE DRIVE
NEW YORK 27, N.Y.

25th January 1949

The exams are now over. I do not yet know anything about my results. It seems very strange to be writing about American affairs, rather than English, and I am not nearly so *au-fait* yet. Quite naturally, it is easier to write of one's native country about which you hear exclusively all your life. As there are no classes now, we will take the opportunity of seeing a few of the plays which are now on in town.

On Thursday, we were not able to hear or see much of inauguration day because of exams, however on Thursday night I went to see *Gone with the Wind*, which is certainly a marvellous picture, and gives a good picture of the 'old South', in the days when a plantation was even more aristocratic than an English country estate. Then of course, it is all destroyed by the civil war, and the film drags a bit, as the last part is just a tumultuous love affair followed in its various stages. But it is a good picture.

On Friday, I worked all day, and then read about the inauguration. The news movies of it were good, but were not nearly so complete as England would probably have had for a Royal event of similar importance.

I spent the afternoon downtown on Saturday, with Bob Andress looking for a corduroy jacket. Eventually I decided I was not so keen on them, so I decided to get Churchill's *Gathering Storm*, plus a silk maroon and paisley tie.

We then went to a Doubleday book and record shop, and played over the album of records *I can Hear it Now*, edited by Ed Munrow, Columbia University (MM800 I think). It is formed of the most famous speeches of this generation put forth as originally recorded. It contains Roosevelt (1st inaugural, Faila and Malta, Funeral Procession); Churchill (Finest, Ship of State); Duke of Windsor (Abdication); Wendell Willkie and Roosevelt's funeral procession, and speeches by many other famous people. In some way I shall have to buy it. If it is not to be published in England, I shall try to bring the album over with me as it is such an historic thing to have.

After working on Saturday evening, on Sunday I went to church in the morning with the Diehls at the Little Church around the Corner. Then we had oysters and calves' brains for lunch at the Lafayette, both of which I thoroughly enjoyed.

On Sunday afternoon I read; followed by a lecture on American literature here at the House, and a harpsichord concert by Ralph Kirkpatrick at the Town Hall which was excellent. He played the *Goldberg Variations* by Bach, and some Scarlatti, which was notable insofar as being one of the sonatas, it nevertheless was in fact more Spanish Royal Procession and Hunt than anything. Afterwards we had a delicious concoction at a nearby restaurant called 'Old Fashioned Strawberry Peach Shortcake', as its name suggests it consisted of Strawberries and Peaches, with cream and shortcake.

Last night we saw a review called *Inside the USA*, with Beatrice Lillie, whose movements are really cute, but who is left behind by Hermione Giegold and by Joyce Grenfell in my estimation, although I think in a way, she is more famous than either. Today we are going to see the film of Hamlet, and tomorrow, Tallulah Bankhead in *Private Lives*.

Tallulah is quite a character here, there is supposed to be no difference in her performance on or off stage. She is the daughter of a former Speaker of the House of Representatives from Alabama; she is a great friend of Truman's, and told the police just how little she cared for them to get on to the presidential reviewing stand at the inauguration!

Then this Saturday is Chinese New Year's Day, and we shall be taking ourselves to that part of New York known as Chinatown.

At the end of February, David Johnson and I shall be going to the Kinkeads for a weekend, and on my birthday the whole crowd of us is going to see the new musical hit, *Kiss me Kate*, which is absolutely the rage here, and a worthy successor we believe to *Oklahoma*. The 19th was the only day we could get tickets for, so that was rather fortunate. I expect as it is a matinee, we shall dine out afterwards, at which restaurant I do not yet know.

Bob Wallace and I shall be sharing a room from the end of this week, which will be very good indeed.

I've ordered a quantity of shirts in my size from a wholesaler's sale, impeccably vouched for by Kay who says her brother has them. Six for $9.75 against a normal $4 each. If they are unsatisfactory, I can get the money returned, but I think they will be all right.

I enclose a copy of an amusing excerpt from *The New Yorker*, dated January 22nd, 1949:

Conversation

Local lady who was invited to a wedding in England but couldn't go, has received one of those nice little white boxes in which it is customary to send out tiny slices of wedding cake. This one was empty, though, except for a printed note from his majesty's postmaster-general, explaining that, in view of the regulations for bidding unlicensed exporting of food from the British Isles, he had been obliged to remove the contents.

I publish this here, as my Mother made me a birthday cake, and Daddy went to post it from England on January 3rd, only to be told that the export of cake had been prohibited since December 31st. However, all was right, as Mr Town Clerk Peter Clarke, in his capacity as Food Officer, was able to arrange for its pre-dating. So that is why I have such a personal interest in this story!

30. IS SIXTY PARTICULARLY OLD?

500 RIVERSIDE DRIVE
NEW YORK 27, N.Y.

31st of January 1949

Bob and I are now settled into our new abode, a double room, #905. We moved late on Saturday afternoon, in rather a hurry, as we were asked to do so just as we were going out. We like it very much indeed and have been successful in getting a hat stand and an extra chest of drawers, a large two-sided desk, and two bookcases moved into it, for our manifold possessions of all kinds, which enveloped the room, and us, for the first 24 hours! Our beds are arranged in bunk fashion, and I think they will be particularly good that way. Until today they were in two parts, but we had the maintenance join them together which is how they were originally arranged.

The walls are gaily decorated with all sorts of pictures and maps, and we have a radio as well. If you look at the picture of International House, you will note two towers. We look out at the back of the building under the right-hand tower, and one floor opens onto the roof of the right-hand wing of International House.

Last week, I was writing a paper most of the time for Professor Goodrich on 'British and American railways'. It was finished on Saturday morning, with me getting up at 7:30 a.m. to type the final pages of it. With the speed and amateurish-ness of my typing, that is quite an achievement.

Apart from that, the week was given over to holiday before the new semester began today. I registered for that on Saturday and I am doing the Goodrich economics history course again, the Commager, and Miss Kendall's in Social Research. Then I am doing a different one under Professor Lynd and one on 'The Federal system' by Professor McMahon. I shall scout around and may quite easily alter some of them, if I find some which are more attractive to my way of thinking.

I decided to see some plays last week with the last of my money, so on Tuesday afternoon we went to *Hamlet - The Film*, which was really very good, and I think it is marvellous how much they managed to put Shakespeare into it. The final scene where the body is carried off onto the parapets of the castle in the mist, rising upstairs all the time, is particularly good. We followed that by a duck dinner at the Czechoslovak Prada which was simply marvellous.

Wednesday was our turn to see *Private Lives* with Tallulah Bankhead; she created a riot with her every movement, and such laughs and deep husky tones that were regaled to us every now and then.

Then at dinner at the House, I met an Englishman who was in New York for a few days on the way to the University of Illinois, and so we went off to see another play *The Madwoman of Chaillot*, by Jean Giraudoux. This play is French, with Martita Hunt, who played Miss Haversham in Great Expectations, in the same role. It is a comic satire; fantasy; and commentary on the contradictions of life today, so extraordinary and bizarre, yet touching and whimsical. At any rate we enjoyed it and it is making a great hit here.

On Thursday and Friday, I worked all day, and had Norman Topp to dinner here. He is the Old Mid-Whitgiftian who had previously taken me out. On Saturday we dined in Chinatown, and then went to see a film called *The Search*, about displaced and orphaned children of concentration camps in Europe. It was very well acted and very tragic, but a marvellous film. That we followed by another visit to the *Kleine Konditorei* for coffee and cakes.

And so we get to Sunday, after a rather cold night in our new room. I went to Holy Communion at 9 a.m. and Matins at 11 a.m., where the Columbia University Chapel disgraced itself by having the wrong tune to my beloved *Hail to the Lords anointed*, which was dreadful sacrilege!

Then in the afternoon I went to the Carnegie Hall to hear the Philharmonic Symphony concert with Stokowski. Miss Hitchcock, whom I met on the boat, was ill, and lent me her season ticket. They played a modern program including Vaughan Williams latest Symphony, which I really like very much.

We came back to the House for tea, followed by a meeting in commemoration of the death of Gandhi. Then Bob and I were invited out to dinner by Mrs Bates, one of the information desk staff here, who seems to approve of us fairly well. She has an apartment near here and gave us lovely ribs of beef. We had a pleasant evening with her and two of her daughters, who are nearly engaged she told us. I made a marvellous remark which caused much merriment.

We were talking about China and Madam Chiang Kai-Shek, whom Mrs Bates said had been at college in the US at the same time as her and was in fact her age. The conversation went on and I, quite uncoordinated and just thinking of Chiang, said "the madam must be getting quite old, about sixty, mustn't she?" You can imagine the laughter. I of course was all apologies as it turns out that they are both forty-eight. I never think of sixty being so particularly old. We had a fine time there and I am now back to work.

I have done quite well in the exams which have now been marked. I got an A minus in Professor Lynd's course, which was wildly better than I expected, and which greatly excited me as I wanted to do well for him. In economic history I got a C, which does not at all please me, as I should have got a B, however it is rather difficult doing the history of a foreign country when everyone else has it as its native history. I shall hope to do better in part two of the course. I got a B in Miss Kendall's Social Research. Professor Commager's course is just a discussion group with no grade, and my Goodrich paper is not yet marked. I am quite pleased altogether. American degrees are granted when a certain number of points are completed, each course is so many points, usually three, and therefore has an exam.

The House's first formal dance of the New Year is on my birthday so we shall follow the theatre and dinner with that; it will be a jolly day. Then one evening Mrs Bates is having a cocktail party, also for my birthday, which I am greatly looking forward to.

I do not know that I shall be in New York at the time of the Rotary convention, as I hoped to manage to get to the west coast at some time, and it would have to be then.

I now have several new shirts; two white; one blue; one fawn; and one green, all for $9.75, plus a pair of dark grey cotton trousers for knocking around in. This is most economical, and they are excellent quality. I needed them and a new tie, dark blue, with a sort of Peacock pattern in white and red, all shot through and very dainty. It was Bob's and we exchanged ties for one that I just bought but like this one of his better, which he disliked.

Today we are back to work, and it has snowed, turned to rain, now the snow has melted, and it has got warmer.

View from room #905 at International house. Photo: John Prior

31. PETITPAS

500 RIVERSIDE DRIVE
NEW YORK 27. N.Y.

February 7th 1949

Bob and I are finding that our room really works out very well indeed. We enjoy the radio from 11 p.m. to 1 a.m., and I am writing this by *Uni to read by*, a very pleasant show broadcast every night from 12 midnight to 1 a.m. and about the best thing that radio here produces. Unfortunately, WQXR and WNYC which are the good stations, have too much interference ever to be reliable.

We now seem to be thoroughly set back in classes, and I think I shall have a busy, but a very profitable, time. Professor Lynd has moved to the problem of 'planning' this term. This week I'm doing a small paper in a seminar on leadership with Doctor Stole as part of the Social Research course on the 'Marxist Connection of the Leader' which is really quite interesting, and which I hope to finish over the weekend. Then I have a lot of reading to do. The typewriter is so usefully employed for papers.

Last Thursday, Bob and I went to see *Anne of the 1000 days* dealing with Anne Boleyn. Not everyone agrees with me, but I think it is excellent; at the least it is colourful. Rex Harrison was marvellous as a thin King Henry VIII. On Friday I went to see the British film *A Canterbury Tale*, which is about the pilgrimage of an American GI to Canterbury.

It was beautifully set, and it was so nice to see that cafe by the gate to the cathedral again, all the countryside so well loved, and the Kentish villages such as Chillingbourne.

On Saturday Bob was in Washington, so I tried out the Petitpas restaurant with Kay Barber, where for dinner we were served hors d'oeuvres; soup; ravioli; ragout of lamb in wine; and figs in Brandy and coffee. We found it to be exceptionally good and so it is where we shall go on my birthday. It is a little French place, and ever so homely and cute.

On Sunday I went to the first Holy Communion said at the Columbia University chapel at 9 a.m. I always go and get their free breakfast afterwards, no toast and marmalade, but doughnuts, coffee, and fruit juice. The chaplain, who is one of the city vicars, is good to talk to. Then I went to Union Theological at 11 a.m. followed by lunch and an inspection of the cafeteria here on behalf of the student council to see if complaints were justified!

I listened to music in the afternoon, and then attended a lecture here by an Iowa farmer, a pretty top one in the US, who was most interesting and knew Britain quite well. On his farm of 440 acres, he employs but three men, and it has livestock of all kinds and vegetables as well as corn so that is some task.

Today I have worked all day, and I am reading about 'religion in America' for Professor Commager's class on Wednesday, which interests me greatly. Reinhold Niebuhr is talking at the House on that subject later in the year, so I shall look forward to hearing him then.

On the 17th of February, I am to fly to Pennsylvania to talk to the Berwick people for Bill Miller, they have a ladies' night, and I am supposed to be humorous! No potted 'your USA' in the dull 'our Croydon' manner, but something rather diamante, and am writing down thoughts as they come. I return to New York the same night by sleeper, so as not to miss classes. It is rather ironical that I should fly, but it is needful with these distances to cover.

On April the 24th I will be going to Atlantic City to speak to a district conference and that too will be enjoyable, then on February the 24th - 26th David Johnson and I are going back up to the Kinkeads for the weekend.

32. CANADIAN RADIO

500 RIVERSIDE DRIVE
NEW YORK 27, N.Y.

14th February 1949

I sometimes feel compelled to adopt the American style a wee, wee bit, just to prove that even a staid and respectable Englishman, slow-witted as are all the 'island people', to quote Churchill, can banter with the wildest products of the wildest state of the wildest West that the western most parts of western democracy has. And by that I do not mean that Californians have no serious side! Hollywood is as much a disgrace to them in their thinking, as it is to civilization as a whole. Nevertheless, letters from Bob's friends are often riots of peculiar semi-demoniac humour, so this is an exercise in that attractive field.

After class last Tuesday morning I went to see the French film *Monsieur Vincent,* which is the story of the life of Saint Vincent De Paul, who lived in France in the 17th century. It is excellent and much better than the so-called religious films that we sometimes have. The churches ought to have taken steps to be able to hire it and rent it out, instead of sermons, for churches that wish it. It is quite moving in the poignant simplicity of its remarkable story of saintly service of the noblest kind.

Afterwards, I ate a nice little steak for lunch at the Champlain restaurant with Bob and Coco, a friend of his from Washington where he was last weekend. She was of Japanese extraction and it later transpired that she was from Milton, Pennsylvania, and that her father had told her all about me when I spoke at the Rotary Club.

She was very friendly with the people with whom I stayed when I was there. All of which is I think a very extraordinary coincidence, and to meet her in New York of all unlikely places!

Then I rated all the travel agencies and proceeded to get all the literature I could about the west US, so that I can begin to decide what I want to do in the summer. I still must see if I can get there, by hook or by crook, by charm or by influence. The rest of the day was 'reading interspersed with food'.

On Wednesday, I was wide awake at 7:45 a.m. to hear Spellmann speak on Cardinal Mindszenty. Spellmann has called the American people to a holy war against communism with no shooting. He of course said all the wrong things, and I am unhappily convinced that the Roman Catholic church sees in this case a heaven-sent way of increasing its worldwide political power and insidious influence. All this talk of 'by host and temple of America' and a war with communism to save American Liberty with its inequalities of wealth and unsolved racial problems ill-becomes a prince of the church. Cardinal Mindszenty was I think reactionary, violent, arrogant, ebullient, and unreasonable all along as he could be, even by Churchillian standards, which doesn't defend but does explain his trial. The intelligent Protestants here think Spellmann is lousy.

On Wednesday evening, the citizens forum of the Canadian Broadcasting Corporation was transmitted from the House. The subject was Marshall Aid, and when the main speakers had finished, a few of ask were able to ask questions for broadcasting. I asked what the effect of depression in America on the economies of the countries receiving aid would be, as that seems to be one of the vital questions. I was probably heard by a lot of people in Canada as the programme is a popular one. I was quite pleased to do it.

On Thursday, I went to the Champlain to lunch again with the little Japanese girl friend of Bob's and it was then that we found out that we were already known indirectly to each other. In the evening there was very enjoyable folk dancing, which I went to for the first time for many weeks.

On Friday, I booked my air passage to Wilkes Barre for this coming Thursday, from Newark in New Jersey. The plane leaves at 2:05 p.m., arriving at 2:45 p.m., and I shall be met by car and return the same night by train. I am quite looking forward to flying.

On Friday evening, I went to the New York debut of Joan Hammond. She had good reviews the next day, and I have never enjoyed a recital of songs and arias so much. She sang many encores, as is the custom here. She had on a white dress with a billowy cape flowing from one shoulder, which became her considerable girth! The audience was most enthusiastic, and the reviews the next day were likewise good.

Together with a Dutchman called Rees Outwater, I went out on Saturday to Montclair in New Jersey on an invitation which the House received. We went to stay with some people called Fradkin. They have a lovely home and Montclair is a very wealthy outer suburb. Mrs Fradkin has just been to Europe to observe the Paris assembly of the United Nations for a group of women's clubs, and she was very typical of that type, but she was most interesting and we both enjoyed our time there. A certain Mrs English had a tea party for a whole lot of students who were being entertained at Montclair during the weekend. Then we had dinner at the Fradkin's and then went to a play in the evening. On the whole in the newer New York theatres, you can see better than in London ones. We finished off with a dance at the cosmopolitan club, and ate chicken at 2 a.m. after the dance, all fingers to the fray!!

On Sunday, we had a marvellous lunch, and talked a good deal, returning to New York in time for the delicious Sunday supper, at which the assistant general-secretary of the UN in charge of economic affairs spoke very well. After that I wrote a few letters before going to bed.

This week, besides the trip to Pennsylvania, there is quite a lot going on, and of course on Saturday my birthday. The arrangements for that are still the same, and I think we shall have an exceptionally good time.

33. MARDI GRAS

500 RIVERSIDE DRIVE
NEW YORK 27, N.Y.

22nd February 1949

(The reader should note that this chapter contains expressions which are reflective of the era in which they were written and are now considered offensive - SMP)

The last three days of the week through Sunday, as the Americans say, were extremely hectic altogether, and then to cap matters off the weather today is humid and relaxing, so I feel like stretching out and going to sleep. Today is a holiday, being the birthday of a distinguished rebel named George Washington. He had something to do with the early history and adolescent disobedience of these parts! Now for some tea and cake, not very English in style, but it is the right time.

My visit to Pennsylvania was on Thursday, when I flew to Wilkes Barre. Flying gave us marvellous views of New York, although the flight was rather bumpy due to high winds, but it was perfectly comfortable, and you get a marvellous panorama of New York as you leave. The plane was a modern Convair, seating about 40 passengers, and the strangest delusion about flying is that you are not apparently going at all quickly, but just struggling along.

Mr Miller met me, and told me that the previous day my photograph had been in the paper! They had a garden night, and I spoke for nearly an hour about one thing and another, including various incidents that have occurred since I was here. I had the usual extravagant comments, and they seemed to laugh when I meant them to.

I returned by night bus and arrived back at the House at 5:45 a.m. after getting quite a lot of sleep on the bus; $28.00 the better off, which pleased me immensely.

I had a lovely birthday which all went off well, and everything combined to give it a festive air. In the morning we had breakfast at about 9 a.m., following which I went shopping for the party that I was to have at 1 a.m. in our room. I also spent some time practising the can-can!

Bob and his helpers were feverishly decorating the auditorium to make it look exotic. Kay, and a lady called Harland; who is one of the staff, went over to Union City and brought back huge steak sandwiches, which we ate in the auditorium as we worked, with dark German beer as a birthday present to me.

Then we went to see *Kiss me Kate*, which is clever, colourful, cute, bright and witty, and the songs particularly in their unexpurgated stage version are really good, ones like *Always True to you in my Fashion*.

There were twelve of us at the Theatre and, joined by Beryl and a friend, we went to the Petitpas, which is a delightful French restaurant and very informal. Dinner was preceded by Dubonnet wine. We were served hors d'oeuvres; onion soup; and ravioli, then baked rabbit and vegetables, ending up with brandied peaches and coffee. We stayed there until about 8 p.m. and returned to the House to get ready for the formal dance, which was quite the best that we have ever had by general agreement.

The theme of the dance was *Mardi Gras*, after the very gay and posh series of balls and festivals which is held each year in New Orleans and culminates on Shrove Tuesday. We had decorated the auditorium to look gay, with mock screen shutters to the windows, hat stands disguised as palm trees, and flowers of paper around the balcony, with balloons and tinsel all over the dark stage curtains. To this was added a soft light.

Everyone thinks that it was quite the best dance that we have had. The highlight of the dance was the floorshow, in which there were three dances. The first was a South American group; then a Negress dancing to jazz; and finally, six boys including me all doing the can-can. We were all properly dressed up for it. Jimi James, who really knows how to do the can-can, trained us, with the result that I shall forever be able to do it.

I think my proficiency in the can-can is an inherited high kicking technique, probably assimilated by me as a wondrous watching infant.

We wore nylons, garters, crepe paper frilly skirts, and vests well filled with paper, with hats over one eye made from those Christmas paper spheres that fold up. The whole time we were on the floor, there was an absolute riot while we danced beneath our highly made-up faces, and we all were adjudged successful. Curtis Green and I were apparently the stars of the six, as we performed with particular gusto! He is very short, so the contrast must have been amazing. It is most exhausting, but I shall never forget the steps, it is really saucy with makeup and odd winks as you dance around.

After the dance, nine of us assembled in our room, and we had a party until 3 a.m. with brandy; sherry; cherry pie; chiffon cake; ginger snaps; cheezits; grapes; bananas; chocolates from Berwick Rotary Club in Pennsylvania; potato crisps; and my mother's marvellous birthday cake. We were Bob Andress; Curtis Green; Rees Outwater; Tony Smith; Nipper; Bill Taylor; Bill Clancy; Bob Wallace; and me.

By superhuman efforts, I was up again at 8:15 a.m. for Holy Communion, and following that, I entertained Helen Carr; Beryl Prendergast; Winkie; Das; Jimi James; Eleanor McRoberts; Kay; and Harland, in the waffle wing at breakfast, and gave them some of the same things. Unless that is done, the girls are left out of parties, as there is no visiting allowed between the sexes in rooms here unfortunately.

I managed to get to church at 11 a.m. followed by a quick lunch; I was in bed reading by 1 p.m.; asleep at 3 p.m.; and awoke at 5:15 p.m. to hear the lecture on the negro question in the Houses *Living America* series.

As Mrs Bates' daughter was ill, the projected party had to be cancelled, but Eleanor and I went to dinner, and I then gave myself a real treat by reading the book on Kent by Richard Church which is so evocative of things well known.

Earlier last week, after seeing Danny Kaye, who I think is much overrated, we had lunch at the Seafare where seafood is magnificent. We had fish *au gratin* such as I have never tasted before in my life.

Today is a horrible day, nasty out and stuffy indoors, so not much fun. Tonight, Otto and I are dining with a man who was a Rotary fellow last year, and on Friday, David and I leave for the Kinkeads.

Bob Wallace, who is 26, though actually you might not think it, is a typical and extremely nice Californian. He is intelligent, and very bright in every respect, quite delightful in fact, and it is said we make a good pair. Rooming together goes as smoothly and as enjoyably as could be. We have similar tastes and senses of humour. He is a Presbyterian, his father's family were mormons of Utah, and his father's cousin's sister was the great founder of Mormonism, Brigham Young's, last and very favourite polygamic wife, Amelia! His mother is a Kansas lady. They live at Exeter in the Central Valley.

Excerpt from the Petitpas brochure.
The citation information of this brochure from the 1940s is unknown.
Please advise if you are the author or know who they are.

34. SLAVERY AND THE SOUTH

SOUTHWOOD

POUGHKEEPSIE, N. Y.

28th February 1949

I am beginning this letter at 11:00 p.m. on Monday night, on the train coming back from Poughkeepsie, where I have stayed an extra day for the food and air in this most delightful of American company. David and I have had a marvellous weekend, and the Kinkeads would take first place in a worldwide contest for good hospitality.

I do not think until you meet the Kinkeads and seen their house in action, you can conceive what they're like at all. I feel the explanation lies in the fact that they are really southerners from Lexington, Kentucky, one of the great centres of southern civilization. That was probably the most gracious society that has existed in the new world, albeit including slavery. There is about the South, and its gentry, something quite like the country class in England.

They run the huge plantations with their slaves, beautiful homes, and tradition, all hospitality of such generosity and size that it is a byword everywhere. I do not yet know all about the slavery question, but of course we began it, and it was English people who enabled it to flourish.

We naturally reject slavery, yet many of the slaves were treated really well, and the owners, and particularly their wives, were as solicitous for their welfare as gentlemen farmers are for their workpeople.

On the average plantation, as in *Gone with the Wind*, the wife was the foundation and director of the domestic economy and she was busy from morning till night. Undoubtedly there were abuses, but in many cases the old South had a charm and grace equal to nothing else in the New World. Allied to this was the grace of their lovely homes, the lavishness of their hospitality, and the magnificence of their cooking, thus it is that the South is the ideal setting for novels, and that southerners are proud, even more so than Kentish men. They look to the confederacy of the civil war as the national glory, even if it was a failure, and venerate Robert E. Lee as no other American is venerated.

It is from that background that the Kinkeads come, and I think it explains the nature of their generosity. They are infinitely kind and can entertain a dozen as easily as one. They are magnificent examples of their type, and so rare now as to be unique.

David and I arrived on Friday evening at 6.00 p.m. and were immediately taken home by the Kinkeads, together with another Englishman, named George Forbes. He hails from Wigan but is now a Canadian citizen. Quite how he became one and what his life history has been I am not too sure, but he seemed extremely pleasant. The Kinkeads met him in 1944, and he is staying with them for a few weeks on vacation, partly working on their estate and partly on holiday.

That day we had three Vassar girls to supper, Annie Garrigue, Alice Davidson, and Kate Breckenridge. They are all nice and we had a huge rich pork pie, which was not home killed, preceded by soup, and followed by ice cream meringues. The sweet potatoes with the pork were candied with bananas, a very delicious flavour.

We then went to see a film about the American Air Force called *Command Decision* starring Clark Gable, which was exceptionally good. The Kinkeads paid for all the tickets. Then we took the girls back to Vassar and returned to the Kinkeads, to the usual pints of milk and cream cake.

The weather was spring-like when we woke up the next morning, not, I regret to say, until 10:30. The Kinkeads refuse to wake up any visiting students, setting out to give them mainly food and sleep if they are thought to need this, which we were! We had a breakfast of porridge and cream, six eggs and bacon, and pints of milk and coffee which filled us up, then we went for a short walk around part of the Kinkead grounds, which stretch one mile deep from the main New York Albany highway to the Hudson River, and are about a quarter of a mile wide. The Hyde Park home of Roosevelt is similar, though larger. The house stands on the edge of a terrace of ground which abruptly ends, and gives way to hilly wooded lands and hills leading to the mighty Hudson.

Returning to the house, we were given soup and steak sandwiches, cakes, orange juice and milk, only being allowed to leave the kitchen with a bright "you'll pass," from Miss Jennie, when our tummies were really podgy.

It was then decided that we should visit Mr Franklin Delano Roosevelt's 'shrine', as they sarcastically called his home and grave. The Kinkeads take all their guests to the gates, pay their entrance fee, leave them there, and pick them up about two hours later. Once again, I found much of very great interest, and for the rest of the weekend, we had great fun in mutual teasing, anything unsavoury will produce a Roosevelt story from them to fit. In their opinion there is no department of human life that the Roosevelt family did not disgrace in some way. But you can at least tease them about him, whereas most Hyde Parkers are far too incensed for that, and as for Truman, well, he should still be selling ties!

On the way back Miss Elise took us to visit Miss Ellen Roosevelt, a cousin of President Roosevelt's who supported him, but is a 'dear friend' of the Kinkeads. She lives in a nice house and made us very welcome, although we could not accept her invitation to tea as we were already late for the sophomore class play at Vassar.

We apparently missed a good part of the play, however we did enjoy what we saw. The songs were catchy, and it was well produced. It was though a little too risqué, modern, and in bad taste for the Kinkeads who were not amused, especially as the girls had written it. They thought the girls knew rather more than they should, and that they hoped none of the girls whom they entertained would ever take part in writing such a play.

As one of the songs in it was *I'm a high-class woman with low aspirations*, perhaps it is not surprising when you come to think of it.

Then that evening, we all went over to the Newtons to dinner and had a fine time and arrived back at Southwood at 1:20 a.m. by taxi. The Kinkeads were already upstairs, but they had left milk and cakes on the hall table. They insist on one thing only, that their guests must be in by 1:30 a.m. They do not retire completely until they are, and they don't think people should keep them up later than that, which is reasonable.

This time, David and I shared the main guest room, as our more usual ones were being spring cleaned by degrees.

On Sunday morning, we arose in time to snatch just a little breakfast and leave with their cousin Miss Cornelia Kinkead for church. The preacher was Doctor Pike, who is to be chaplain to Columbia University, but he is not, I consider, so very great a preacher as Poughkeepsie thinks he is.

The Kinkeads stayed behind to prepare the great picnic for after church, a truly American institution. For this there were three Vassar girls, Alice, Jean, and Connie. We walked down to the cabin in the woods, and there we had a fine feed which we transported from the house and which we greatly enjoyed. The cabin has a large living room and changing rooms for the swimming pool, which is used in the summer. We had hot dogs, spaghetti (cooked in the house), coffee, cake, and various oddments like crackers. With the great wood fire and the trees beyond through the windows it was marvellous.

We had a jolly time, and it was typically American, I think. Then in the rest of the afternoon, we walked down to the Hudson and spent time clambering in their woods and climbing the hills. We returned to the cabin for popcorn, cakes, and marshmallows with coffee. It was all simply perfect in such a memorable day. At the cabin we were joined by three more Vassar girls, named Elizabeth, Mary and Barbara, who were visiting with Barbara's Mother, Mrs Burr. Elizabeth was a high-spirited Mississippi girl of the Scarlet O'Hara kind.

Then our three Vassar girls departed, and the rest remained to supper at Southwood, which was scrambled eggs; salad; vegetables; cakes; milk; coffee; and tea. We played parlour games until 10:00 p.m., after which the girls left, and David went back to New York for classes.

I decided to stay another day for the air and food, as I had no classes and therefore went early to bed and had a long night's rest.

Upon getting up the next morning, I found that it was snowing, which was a shock as I had hoped to experiment with riding one of the Kinkead's horses with George. However, that was not to be, so after a six-egg breakfast, we went for a walk before lunch to eliminate some of the effects of further eggs and cream. Lunch consisted of soup; braised beef and rice; pear and cheese salad; fancy coconut cakes; milk and tea; marshmallows and strawberry ice cream!

In the afternoon following that, George and I walked the half mile or so to their cousins Miss Cornelia's at Maple Grove, as I particularly wanted to see her house, which is even lovelier than Southwood, though it does not lead down to the Hudson. It is built about 1823 or 1843 and is a better style than the Kinkead's house. Inside it has a magnificent staircase, with a furnished landing three steps above hall level, and then goes on up around the sides of a central well.

It is most elegant and has a huge window at its back. The sitting room adjoins the hall, all being really one room. Then there are two smaller sitting rooms, the huge drawing room, a billiard room, and of course kitchens. Everything is beautifully kept and very orderly, the Kinkead house being somewhat of a muddle.

We stayed and had tea with Miss Cornelia, then returned to Southwood and left for the men's church supper where the speaker was an American businessman who has a refrigeration plant in England. He thought he had been treated well by the government when he could prove that the firm was going to export goods and he did not think that iron and steel should be nationalised. But I do not think many Englishmen in business see things quite so clear headedly as he did. The Kinkeads met us from that, and here I am now on the train.

I had such a marvellous weekend altogether, and it is so good to have such friends and of course I think they enjoy it too. But I think they are an exceedingly rare type and remarkably kind to everyone they know. Jeannie Kinkead, for example, spent most of Sunday with a sick old woman on their farm, and last year they took warm cow's milk to a friend who needed it. For weeks they delivered it at 8 a.m. each day, saying it was no trouble at all.

Group in front of the Kinkead's cabin. L-R: Unknown, unknown, unknown, George Forbes, unknown, Annie Garrigue, David Johnson, John Prior, unknown. Photo: John Prior

35. I'LL GET DRUNK WHEN ROOSEVELT DIES

500 RIVERSIDE DRIVE
NEW YORK 27, N.Y.

6 March 1949

On Friday, I went to a small Rotary club at West Orange, a suburb next to Montclair, to speak at their luncheon. I spoke on England at the present time, and gave a good account of the economic situation, explaining that standards of living in rationed foods could only be raised when we were economically secure. In the afternoon, I visited the Edison laboratories and library, and saw where Edison lived and worked, all in West Orange.

I stayed there overnight with a young Rotarian who had two small children, a boy of six and a girl of two, both of whom were rather sweet. They were interesting company, and we had a hectic evening. Their Democratic brother-in-law and sister, who had been appearing at Drury Lane in *Oklahoma*, and the Rotary club secretary and his wife joined us, and there were simultaneous stimulating arguments all going at once about BBC versus American radio; Roosevelt versus Republican; whether Great Britain's people were getting much extra from Marshall aid; or use far more food in Great Britain, with dry martinis as referees and encouragement. I returned to New York after lunch on Saturday.

Here is another little bit of Roosevelt demonology I discovered while in West Orange. One Rotarian to whom I was talking at lunch, made it his proud boast that he had vowed with all his friends to get drunk in celebration when Roosevelt died. As soon as his wife told him of the great man's passing, off he joyously went to a jubilant celebration on April 12th 1945 and did as planned!

That was the second time I had heard that, apparently it was quite notorious in the snootier places in Manhattan. I do not however think that was a countrywide reaction, even among his opponents, but feeling is apparently particularly bitter in the Hudson Valley and East as a whole. I think the fundamental complaint against Roosevelt is twofold; they think his policies were socialistic, the turn against rugged individualization, and far more bitterly in a Kinkead case, that he and Mrs Roosevelt were both egalitarian in their social relations, and though of course they boast that America has no classes at sometimes, at others they think he just betrayed them, by suggesting that their importance was so great after all.

The rest of the weekend consisted of a Chinese dinner on Saturday, followed by the Ginger Williams play *Night Must Fall* at the House, which was excellently done, and in which Beryl Prendergast once again distinguished herself. She is to play Elvira in *Blithe Spirit* in the House on April the 5th.

After that Mr Mastude, the education officer here, gave a family party in his apartment for the cast, and I went along for an hour or so. Then I went with Bob, Bogie and another friend, down to the *Kleine Konditorei* and retired rather later than perhaps I should have done.

On Sunday, I went to the Little Church around the Corner with the Diehls, but not to lunch as they had a previous engagement. Mr Diehl has invited me to talk for ten minutes on April 5th to the annual meeting of the New York Rotary Club, the subject is to be 'What is the Value of the Fellowships?' I shall have to prepare everything carefully, to make the best use of the few minutes.

Then on a beautiful Sunday afternoon, Bob Andress and I went out with Kay in her car for a country drive. We were back in time for a very poor talk on American business, following which I went with David Johnson to dinner with the Reverend Daniel and Mrs Jenkins. He is now studying up at Union Theological College, and we donated him the ham that the Kinkeads had given us.

Mr Jenkins is the assistant editor of the Christian newsletter and is here on a Commonwealth fellowship. We had a remarkably interesting time. They are good people, and have two children, both over here.

Today, I have written letters and done quite a variety of laundry. I have successfully used liquid starch that you dilute with water and dip in before putting in the dryer, to starch collars and cuffs, just to crispen them up a little. For the past month I have sent some shirts out because I did not have an opportunity to launder, but economy is coming back! Tonight, we had free tickets to a play called *My Name is Ajilon*, which was French, and enjoyable, and then we had coffee and strawberry pie.

In general, everything still seems to be going swimmingly well, and it only needs 48 hours in a day to make life perfect. I do as much as I can in those hours that there are, and the whole place seems evermore like home. The money seems to be working out very well. At the student deposit bank, we can only withdraw once a week, which induces a salutary measure of planning and forethought to large purchases. This has probably saved me a lot of money, as I do not carry too much around with me. I shall I think be able to squeeze enough to get to the west coast in June.

Next Sunday we have some Vassar girls coming to International House for the day, so we shall have to be charming and gracious. The lobby here has just had new green tile carpets and walls a treat, as the saying goes. It is cold this week, so my pyjamas have been brought out again for a little.

36. MADISON SQUARE GARDENS

500 RIVERSIDE DRIVE
NEW YORK 27, N.Y.

14th March 1949

I have had quite an interesting few days, chiefly occupied in finishing a paper on 'great men in history', which I shall type later today.

On Friday evening, about fourteen of us went to the 86th Street Brauhaus, which is a German restaurant of the traditional Bavarian kind. Mr Jaeger, the Union City Baker, was coming, but at the last moment he could not. We had an excellent time, with good food. After we had finished dining, we began to dance hectically to the little *Schnitzel Bank* (band) and whizzed around in a restricted space.

There was also a floor show, and then we went afterwards over to our favourite *Kleine Konditorei* for coffee and cakes, all of which was a little costly. The German beer they served there was more like brown ale than anything else that I have tasted here.

Kay was going upstate for the weekend, so Bob and I went for another drive in her car as it was a lovely day, we came back to New York by train and called on Mr Jaeger to order the strawberry shortcake he will be making for celebrating Kay's birthday on March 24th. He took us to have beer and delicious steak sandwiches, which was excellent and kept us filled for the rest of the day.

After returning to the House, in the evening we explored the antiques fair at Madison Square Gardens. This was rather like an outsize second-hand market. All the various shops displayed their wares on stands there. There were some lovely things; we enjoyed browsing and there were many items that I should have liked.

We emphasised the 'fair' part by having our profiles cut, which I think is quite good, and by having our handwriting read. The woman was surprisingly accurate with us both, and although I think their statements are made in such a way that you can read what you will into them by emphasising any of several phrases, I think there is some basis for what she says.

The woman thought that mine showed a mind always on the go, charity, detachment, energy, but a little too conservative and cautious! I also bought a $10 Confederate bill of civil war days for $1. This was money that was to be honoured after the civil war, it will be an interesting memento to have.

On Sunday I went to church at 9 a.m. and 11 a.m., and then six of us had Vassar girls here for the day in a kind of return visit. They certainly seemed to appreciate seeing the House and liked it very much indeed. I am not surprised as it is a most attractive place. They arrived just after I had returned from church. We had lunch, took them over the House and chatted while I played the piano in the House room which they greatly admired, so I suppose my limited playing does not sound too bad!

We then went out for a walk to Grant's tomb, and to Columbia University, returning to the House for an exceptionally fine display of Indian dancing. At 5 p.m. we went to Riverside church to an organ recital there, then we all went to Sunday supper, at which Miss Das, who lives at the House, spoke very well. Mr Mott very kindly took the girls to that as guests of the House and gave them a special welcome, so they felt that they were being made a fuss of, which doubtless flattered them!

Yesterday, via an invite which came through International House, I spent the day about forty miles north of here at Yorktown Heights, speaking to various classes at a rural high school and seeing how everything was run, which was beneficial for me and showed up the differences between English and American schools in considerable detail.

Overall, I'm not sorry to have been educated in England. I think that high schools are as different as can be, more like the modern secondary schools and run most informally. Afterwards I had dinner with the master who invited me.

Since returning, I have been working and I am now looking forward to a nice long night's rest, as I have no early classes tomorrow.

Beryl Prendergast has been offered and accepted an engagement to tour this summer playing leads in two plays with a repertory company in New England. It is an incredibly good thing for her, they asked her after seeing her act here. The time seems to be flying!

37. THE GREAT PARADE OF ALL THE IRISH

500 RIVERSIDE DRIVE
NEW YORK 27, N.Y.

21st March 1949

I have had another week hard at work for this round of Rotary talks, to be given during April. I think I finished typing my paper on Wednesday, and then Thursday being St Patrick's day, I went to watch the great parade of all the Irish that lasts from noon until dark up 5th Avenue. For the first time I wondered if it was wise to exhibit my English accent and decided it might not be. It was most impressive, but lacked crispness; nevertheless, it was something quite different from anything that we have ever seen in England. We then had a Chinese dinner and I followed that by writing the round letter.

     On Friday evening, there was a dinner of the New York chapter of the International House alumni in New York. We all made little speeches on what we thought of things. One of the Nigerians, who I like personally very well, made a violent speech about the British enchaining the poor African natives. This kind of thing always brings out this unions part in me abroad, that as a kind of representative you adopt a 'my country, right or wrong' attitude, which I really think is bad, but which I find myself slipping into.

I am not sure where my opinions really are on this matter. If the colonies say they want their freedom, and would rather stew in their own juice than be stewed by us, what can you say, except all right. I think that we must do a great deal very quickly about our colonies and grant them much more freedom. Even though I think that much we do can be defended, it frequently looks as though it is only for our economic benefit.

On Saturday we went out to dinner at a good place called The Golden Eagle where we had very tasty 'Chicken a la Cacciatora'.

Then on Sunday, Reinhold Niebuhr preached the best sermon I have yet heard him preach, on the temptations of Christ and what they mean for this age. He certainly has a remarkable brain and a very penetrating and brilliant delivery. He draws a large crowd and is, I am convinced, quite without parallel; he finds so much in everything.

38. THE PICKETING OF THE WALDORF-ASTORIA

500 RIVERSIDE DRIVE
NEW YORK 27, N.Y.

28th March 1949

(The reader should note that this chapter contains expressions which are reflective of the era in which they were written and are now considered offensive - SMP)

It is spring out and glorious weather. Last Tuesday, for my course in social research I had to obtain three interviews from residents as part of a housing survey of one of the poorer parts of New York, though not in Harlem. We had a choice of twenty apartments, and I was successful in gaining admission to three of them so that I could do the interviews.

    Rather to my surprise, the women I interviewed were quite cooperative, and they answered the considerable twelve-page string of questions very well. I had general conversation with them as I went along, of course, which made it quite a revelation of how some of the poorer people in New York live, although these were not the poorest. Nevertheless, I think New York is a bad place for bringing children up in as there is no open space for most.

    On Wednesday we were to have a House debate on Africa, and so, in order to know what Great Britain had done in her colonies, and our policies and performances, I went down to the British Information Services to get some information.

I then remembered that ex-Alderman Frank Mitchell of Croydon was now assistant director of the press and radio section there, and of course one of the best men ever to sit in Katherine Street. Remembering too that when he left he said he should be pleased to see Croydonians, I went and called on him. He seemed most happy to see me, and we talked generally and got on very well. Amazingly he recognised me as one of the people he had given a speech making prize to, and he recalled several Croydon youth functions.

Then he took me out to lunch at the oyster bar of the News Centre restaurant in the Rockefeller Centre, where British Information Services is situated. So altogether it was a very pleasant affair, and we talked mainly about Croydon. He thinks he could take up Croydon affairs again just as if he had never left the town. He was very interested in the International Language club in Croydon, but he had not seen International House here, so I invited him to inspect it.

That afternoon, Professor Commager was reasonably good in his class and kept us all remarkably amused by all that he said about Teddy Roosevelt, Franklin Delano Roosevelt, and America's constitution.

On Thursday it was Kay's birthday, and I bought her a little sort of paperweight ornament in metal, of a cook at a big old-fashioned stove, nicely coloured. I went out to dinner with her and her mother at the tea garden rooftop Butler Hall, a big apartment block near here, with a fine view over the city of New York. This was followed by folk dancing in the evening, which I love.

On Friday we went to see the picketing of the Waldorf-Astoria conference on peace, to which the Britons were refused admission by the visa section of the state department, as they make the ridiculous complaint that it is a communist set up. I can believe anything of that department's ineptitude after last summer's journeys to Grosvenor street. The picketing aimed to have 20,000 people around the hotel, but it did not seem to be that passionate. The state department and the press would have done far better to have left the meeting alone, and then it would not have been influential.

That evening, Bob and I, together with one or two other people from the House, were invited to a party the Motts were giving in their apartment for their teenaged children and their friends. They have a big enough room for dancing, together with plenty of delicious refreshments. We thought it was nice of them to ask us to a private party of theirs. At the end of the party, we heard that two International House people were engaged rather unexpectedly.

On Saturday, I spent the afternoon with Maeve McPeek, as her parents were visiting New York, they paid for me, which was genuinely nice. We first went to the Museum of the City of New York, which sets out in graphic form the history of this city, together with whole rooms reproduced from its old homes like those of the Rockefellers with china, glass, silver, and furniture, all just up my street!

Then we went for a ride around Central Park in a hansom cab, which is one of the things to do, especially in spring weather of 75 degrees such as we are currently enjoying. We then went and had dinner at the Sea Fare restaurant. I had lemon sole *au gratin* and it was delicious in every respect. We finished up by going to Radio City Music Hall, where the floor show was much better than usual, and where the film *Little Women* was also good, and quite true to the story, according to Maeve. It was nice to see her again, although impossible to find time to visit her for a weekend.

On Sunday, I went to church with the Diehls and then out to lunch with them to Barbetta's, where we were served *zabioque* for dessert which is whipped white of egg and Sherry. After that we went to see the film *Easter Parade*, which is colourful and gay and has exceptionally good music.

Mr Diehl was telling me that he had achieved fifty years' service in Masonry last year. He apparently retired in 1934 and has since only maintained a small office from which he does unpaid work for the traffic commissions. Traffic, highways, and public works were his speciality and his engineering firm employed 300 trained engineers with branches in Mexico City, Florida, two in Canada, and all over New York State.

That afternoon, I went with a group from the House to Father Divine's church in Harlem. He has a controversial religious movement there and his followers worship him as if he is God. He is a negro of 71, and I think that he gains respect by making the poorest negroes feel that they have some dignity left.

I think he sincerely helps many of them to be better people, but on the other hand, many people feel that he is a crook. I do not exactly know how large is following his, but it is quite considerable among some sections of the negroes.

There are all sorts of women in hysterics or ecstasies, lots of shouting, singing by a very rhythmical choir, also an address by Father Divine all of which was very interesting.

Everyone there has a huge meal of food blessed by him, for which you pay fifteen cents up, so we all gave a dollar. Nine different vegetables are served; then salads; then fish; then meats and poultry; then pies; cakes; cookies comity; then desserts; iced tea and ice coffee; and ice cream. That is his way of showing that there is a world of plenty. One of the sayings is 'so glad, father', so we said, "so full, father," but although it is easy to laugh, I think that we are wrong to do so because in actual fact he is doing something useful, but only, I think, because the regular church fails.

I have got quite a few arrangements made for Easter now. On Saturday 9th April, I am leaving New York to spend the weekend with Kay at her home in Fredonia near Buffalo. She is driving up there, so that will be marvellous and is exceedingly kind of her.

Then Bill Glenn, who I met in England last summer, sent me an invitation for the Easter vacation, so on Tuesday or Wednesday I shall go straight from Buffalo to Virginia and stay with him in Virginia Theological College, Alexandria from April 12th or 13th until Easter Monday. It is genuinely nice of him to invite me; I was so glad to get his letter; and we shall be close enough to Washington to take that in thoroughly as well. Then I go straight from there to the Rotary district conference at Carlisle, Pennsylvania, near Harrisburg, where I am to give a talk on Tuesday morning, and then return to New York.

I had a letter from the Rotarian in California whom I met on the Marine Juniper, asking me what I intended doing about a trip there, and saying that if a Rotary district sponsored me, and I agreed to speak to them, I should be able to get my travelling expenses paid. That sounds quite promising. Thus, I shall hope to leave New York about May the 27th and go to Chicago for a night, three nights in Utah with Bob's aunt, and then to California for three weeks, and back via the Grand Canyon and New Orleans to New York at the beginning of July. Then I shall have the week in New York before sailing, to wind up those of my affairs here still outstanding.

I also had an invitation today from Rotary International, to go to the United Nations at Lake Success, New York. They give all the fellows the option of going as UN interns for two months to see how it works and assist in the work of a part of it. That would be from July to September, but of course I do not think my deferment lasts, and with my return passage booked, I don't think I shall attempt to change it. Also New York is so very hot in the summer.

Today I heard Reinhold Niebuhr talk on foreign policy. He was his brilliant self, although I could not agree with much that he said, and I think he speaks with insufficient knowledge of the facts. He is in high spirits and goes on after dinner conversation rather too much I fear, something dear Billy never did. He met Churchill, and quotes him as saying 'we only need, gentlemen, to remember sufficient of the past to be creative for the future', which is rather good.

Mr and Mrs Diehl and their Son outside Barbetta's Restaurant. Photo: John Prior

39. ARE AMERICAN TEENAGE GIRLS LIKE ENGLISH ONES?

500 RIVERSIDE DRIVE
NEW YORK 27. N.Y.

April 6th 1949

It was such an honour to be the main speaker at the New York Rotary Club annual business meeting tonight, and I was a little apprehensive. I could not really settle to anything, either last night or today, except to prepare for the speech, and I was a little more on tenterhooks than usual. However now it is over, and I think it was one of my more resounding successes. It was shorter than my other speeches, at only fifteen minutes, but I delivered it word for word, and as I had to bend to a microphone fixed in the desk it was well that I had prepared it carefully.

I spoke at a high level about the value of the interchange of students, and of general principles, opportunities, dangers, and experiences of this, rather than the more controversial tone which I usually adopt. I had the usual nice thanks, and an invitation out to Westchester County for a weekend which I shall take up. The meal there was excellent; grapefruit; bean soup; a superb chicken; peas and potatoes; and ice pudding and petits fours for dessert. Otto Borch, the other Rotary fellow, was there to watch me, and highly approved.

Just before the meeting, and having previously decided that my financial position was rosy, I decided to end the pyjama set up and buy a couple of pairs. It is all right here to improvise, but with all the visiting I must do, the measure of comeliness is appropriate. I went to Lou and Fay Lowe's and got two pairs for $5.50 each, not bad! They are poplin fabric, one purple and turquoise bound in lemon; the other grey bound with maroon. Although they are plain colours, they are very smart and extra-long and therefore excellent. I am quite pleased and can therefore throw away the old ones completely.

Now to return to the beginning of the week. It seemed quite like home with Laski lecturing at Columbia University. In true vintage Laski, he spoke with every mannerism slightly exaggerated, to impress the large and uninitiated audience. He gave a brilliant presentation, with the usual never-ending sentences. In answering questions, he just put on a virtual debating show, which I thought was a shade too much overdone. He is so devastating, witty and scathing to quite sensible questions, as if he were engaging in life-or-death debate. One gem was, "if the questioner will read the chapter in my book 'The American democracy on trade unions', he will find the answer with equal profit to himself and myself."

As a lecturer, he is streets ahead of most things here. He has been banned from speaking in California University, and in public school halls in Cambridge, Massachusetts. It is all very stupid of the Americans to think that they can preserve their Democratic liberties from the danger of communism, by denying them in practise.

Wednesday was a lovely spring like day, and I spent the morning walking and talking on Riverside Drive, followed by Professor Commager's class, and then got down for the rest of the week to attending to my complicated affairs and typing the report to Rotary International.

Later in the week, I had quite an interesting time, talking to girls of thirteen to fifteen years old, who were members of the youth builder club of a school in Puerto Rican Harlem. This club, which meets once a week, is concerned with citizenship. They discuss week by week some big topic, and they invite people to come along and answer their questions on various matters.

I answered all their questions on England and I greatly enjoyed my time there, as I think did they.

We were quite homely; discussed cricket; afternoon tea; pounds shillings and pence; as opposed to cents, nickels, dimes, quarters, and dollars; which they found quite complicated. They were most keen to know whether English girls of their age were like them. My answer was, "yes, pretty much!"

That night we had a meeting of the Commonwealth Committee for the Spring Folk Festival here, on April the 30th. I conducted the meeting, but I am now withdrawing as I have too much else to do, such a programme is easier conceived than delivered. The rest of the day was spent in reading and writing letters to the various clubs I am speaking for, and getting the report and letters sent to Rotary International.

On Saturday morning, I had a class at which I was able to talk about Churchill and his story quite a good deal, and then returned to the House for lunch. In the afternoon I went to hear Edith Weissman play the harpsichord. She is middle aged, and has a very stately, German, and military walk, and a dress that rustled so much that I thought it must be announcing 'rustle of spring'. She played some rather descriptive little pieces that I found peculiarly attractive, including a delightful thing called *The King of Denmark's Galliard* by John Dowland. After that, it being Rees Outwater's birthday, he took us to a cocktail lounge on the Avenue, where we naturally had cocktails.

David Johnson and I then caught the train for Poughkeepsie at Grand Central; the Kinkeads paying the fare from their family ticket which was due to expire today. I arrived to the usual sumptuous welcome dinner at 8 p.m; chicken and rice, salad, twenty halves of peaches and meringues. After dinner we sat and talked and played cards and retired early to bed.

We were up at 10 a.m. in time for breakfast, not the usual six eggs, just two sausages and porridge and cream. Church was at 11.05 for 10:45(!). It was communion, so we arrived for the excellent sermon by Doctor Pike. I was more impressed by him than previously. He is to be the new chaplain to Columbia University, which is an important job.

The whole Kinkead estate was looking beautiful. There were daffodils and harebells through the woods and Forsythia on the banks. I have taken some snapshots.

Church was followed by one of the lavish Kinkead picnics, with some Vassar girls. We had roast beef and potatoes, followed by fruit and tomato juice and doughnuts. We mistook the dessert, supposed to be chocolate tapioca, for sandwich spread, and were therefore made to eat a lot when got back to the house and told the Kinkeads what had happened!

In the evening, we broke all records by getting the Kinkeads and ourselves early to the Garrigue's for dinner. Mrs Garrigue nearly fainted with astonishment, but it was vital to be on time as we were returning to New York that same night. We had a delightful time at the Garrigue's, and they have an extremely cute home, the lounge is mostly different greys, set off by pink and green and they have a grand piano.

On Monday, I was preparing my speech, seeing the North Atlantic pact signed on television, and listening to a very brilliant talk on existentialism here in the House.

This Friday, I am going to hear Bruno Walter conducting Beethoven's 5th and 6th symphonies. Then at 6 a.m. on Saturday, I will leave with Kay and four others for Fredonia, via Buffalo, where I shall stay until Wednesday. I will then continue down to Bill Glenn's to stay at Virginia Theological College at Alexandria six miles from there until Monday, when I proceed to the Carlisle district conference for two days including their Governors Ball, and a banquet in the evening. I will leave early Wednesday, in time to get the train back to New York for Professor Commager's class.

Cabin in the woods by the lake on the Kinkead estate. Photo — John Prior.

40. A POSTCARD FROM LIMA

Postcard sent by John Prior, text as below.

Jean's deluxe cabins and restaurant
Routes 5 and 20
Lima NY

4:15 p.m. Saturday 9th April
The owners of this are English; left Lowestoft 2 years ago.

We departed New York at 6:00 a.m. this morning and are now 70 miles from Buffalo, and 110 miles from Kay's Home at Fredonia. Have had a glorious drive and seen Cornell University.

John *(also signed by Rees Outwater, Kay Barber, Stan Prosser and one other).*

41. HERE THE BRITISH COME!

500 RIVERSIDE DRIVE
NEW YORK 27, N.Y.

20th April 1949

I have had the most wonderful and varied time in Fredonia; Washington; Williamsburg; and Alexandria. With Kay Barker; Rees Outwater; and three other people, we left the House on Saturday April 9th at 6 a.m. and arrived 350 miles away in Buffalo in the evening. We had lunch midway at a place run by people only two years out of England; a strange coincidence.

The drive was glorious; first of all, through mountains, and then through fertile valleys, up to Ithaca and Cornell University, with its famous gorges, and on past the Finger Lakes of New York State. Buffalo is a large industrial town of 800,000 people on Lake Erie. Kate lives at Fredonia, an attractive town 50 miles past Buffalo and three miles from the Lake. We arrived there by 7:30 p.m., which was particularly good time.

John Prior and Rees Outwater outside Jeans Deluxe Cabins and Restaurants, Lima, New York. Taken at lunchtime, Saturday April 9th 1949. Photo: John Prior

In the morning, I went to Holy Communion at 8 a.m., and then to the Methodist Church at 11 a.m. The sermon was particularly good, and there was a huge congregation. In the afternoon, we went to Kay Barber's family cabin, by a lake seven miles away, where they spend a lot of time in the summer. It is an American custom for the middle class to have these lake cabins. In the evening, we visited an English woman who has made a fortune in high class sweets, and then went to hear a cantata for Lent.

Monday was my only late morning in bed. I had lunch and breakfast combined, and came downstairs at 11:30 a.m. It was a glorious day, and, in the afternoon, we drove into Buffalo to visit the greenhouses of the park. Then we travelled on to Niagara Falls, a not over-rated sight. The Niagara River flows placidly along, then suddenly begins to gather momentum, goes over rocks, divides in two around an island and crashes down to the whirlpool beneath, throwing up spray higher than itself, and making a wonderful sound.

In the evening, we had dinner at the Restaurant in the Ansley Wilcox House, where Teddy Roosevelt took the oath of office as President after McKinley's assassination in Buffalo in 1901. McKinley was attended to before he died by my Rotary friend Mr Diehl's father, as mayor and physician. I went to bed early, to get up for the 450-mile journey to Washington.

I arose at 5:30 a.m. on Tuesday, April the 12th, to have breakfast and be at the station by 6:30 a.m. to catch the train to Washington. The journey began travelling past the vine and farming country of Western New York, and then through the Catskills and other mountains, down through the Susquehannock Valley, past the places like Lockhaven and Milton that I have previously visited. We paused briefly in Harrisburg, then continued through Pennsylvania and Maryland, where the countryside resembled that of England, particularly Kent. I arrived in Washington at 8:40 p.m. and was met by Bill Glenn and a friend of his.

We drove through Washington which is a well-planned city. The main buildings are floodlit vistas, including the Dome of the Capitol, the White House, and the mansion of General Robert E. Lee in Arlington National Cemetery. Its white columns are suspended above Washington overlooking the Potomac River. Virginia Theological College, where I was staying, is in Alexandria, six miles from Washington. It is an old building with large rooms.

I arose uncomfortably early at 7:00 a.m. to a wet day. I was given a lift into Washington, I had some breakfast, and then went and joined the group from International House who were staying in the city and had arranged a coach to see the sights. We started by seeing the half-completed and exceptionally beautiful gothic cathedral of Washington, and the various embassies, of which the British is one of the nicest and finest. Then we toured on to the Jefferson and Lincoln memorials. The former is a circle of columns with a portico and statue, and the latter is a massive affair. Motoring slowly through Alexandria, we saw all the old houses, including the home of John Lewis, which is exceptionally large.

Then we drove on to Washington's residence at Mount Vernon, where we had a traditional American meal of baked Virginia ham and cherry pie. Washington was a rich man, and the Great Grandfather (by his wife's first husband), of General Robert E. Lee. Mount Vernon is a lovely House overlooking the Potomac, and has white wooden columns facing a park, leading down to the Riverside.

The wings curve outwards and curtain the domestic offices, and there is a large lawn in front. Just now all the azaleas, magnolia, dogwood, and trees are blooming, and the whole of the South is looking so stunning. It is covered with green and freshness, which is later shrivelled by the sun, more so than in England. The House inside at Mount Vernon is supposed to be typical of its period and type.

Following that, we visited the Lee mansion at Arlington, high on a hill overlooking Washington. Originally it belonged to the Washington and Curtis families, and was built in about 1800. In 1831, Robert E. Lee, later to command the Confederate (or southern) forces in the civil war, and a remarkable Christian, soldier and person, married the daughter Mary Curtis, and thus the house and its 11,000-acre plantation became their magnificent home. It has fine gardens, and the members of the household were noted for their lavish hospitality. In the civil war the property was confiscated for non-payment of taxes, and the whole acreage became a burial ground.

After the war, it was returned to the Lee children, who never occupied it, selling it back to the government. Since then it has become the Arlington National Cemetery, and many famous people are buried there. Having watched the changing of the guard at the tomb of the unknown soldier, we went back to Washington. After dinner, I met Bill and we heard Brahms *Requiem* at the Church of Saint John which was where Franklin Delano Roosevelt and Winston Churchill went at Christmas 1942.

On Thursday, I had arranged to visit Williamsburg for two days. Williamsburg is the colonial capital of Virginia and has been restored to its former glory by Mr Rockefeller. In the past twenty years, he has acquired 98% of the town, and has rebuilt three main streets as they were. He has also built a couple of hotels, the Williamsburg Inn and the Lodge. Everybody said I should visit it, and the ever-faithful Kinkeads had given me the address of some friends of theirs who live there. So, I wrote to them, and said that I should like to stay.

They run their house for visitors, although, as I found out, they are very original inhabitants. I left Alexandria at 9:30 a.m. and travelled by train to Richmond, where I met Margaret Lucas, a girl from the House, and drove around with her, seeing a little of the town while eating a picnic lunch.

The Capitol there is magnificent, and the main heroes of the confederacy are commemorated on Monument Avenue, certain people touching their hats to General Lee as they pass him. Richmond has fine houses, and out in the rich neighbourhoods the long azalea and dogwood-lined drives, with lawns and trees leading up to the stately white columned houses, seemed out of *Gone with the Wind*.

From Richmond, I continued my train journey on to Williamsburg. It was such a beautiful day, and I was immediately charmed by the whole place. It is all restored as it would have been in 1720, and intact without later additions, so it shows architecture in this period more completely than any place in England. There are three main streets in Williamsburg, of which the chief is the Duke of Gloucester, named after Queen Anne's son. The streets are lined not only by houses of the period, but by the taverns, in which the plantation owners stayed during 'publick times' if they did not own a town house. In the Raleigh Tavern, Washington, Jefferson, and Patrick Henry ate, and in the Capitol many of the famous features of the revolution were made.

I then went to find the home of the Misses Morecocks, with whom I was to stay. Their house, the Benjamin Waller House, is one of the original ones. They are between 60 and 70 years old, and named Miss Agnes and Miss Pinky! They made me very welcome and invited me to stay as their guest free of charge, and in general were very complimentary. In the evening I went to see the educational film about the city, and saw some of the town by moonlight. Miss Kitty presented me her home-made strawberry ice cream, after which I retired early to bed.

The Benjamin Waller house, Williamsburg, residence of Misses Kitty, Aggie and Pinky Morecocks. They lived there and made ice cream. Photo: John Prior

I rose early on Good Friday, and after breakfast I set out to see the town. Away to the left of the Duke of Gloucester street is the Governor's Palace, an elaborate version of what might be called a 'middling house', with a gracious ball and supper rooms at the back. The governor's rooms are far more luxurious than those for the colonial people, which caused an over bejewelled and flashly-dressed woman in my tour group to remark upon the pretentiousness of the English and the simplicity of the Americans. The whole is surrounded by gardens of that period, and every fitting and furnishing of the house is beautiful and authentic, and mostly brought from England.

I then attended the Good Friday service at Bruton parish church. It was like English churches, with an elaborate pew for the Royal Governor and brass candelabra. I had lunch at Chownings Tavern, and then in the afternoon continued to view old buildings where the public is shown around by guides in 18th century dress. The taverns there are more like the English public houses than anything else here. The College of William and Mary has the oldest college building in America, and is reputedly designed by the great Sir Christopher Wren.

The gardens at Williamsburg, having only the original flowers and box hedges in them, giving them that unique smell, are perhaps the loveliest feature of America. It is a fact that the English garden; country or suburban; is rare in America, where the summers are too hot, and the winters are too cold, so those at Williamsburg are therefore all the more appreciated. Unfortunately, I had to leave at 4 p.m., but I had really been able to see most of the things in Williamsburg of greatest interest, and to be captivated by the charm of all its houses both public and private.

On the return journey, I had dinner in Richmond, and was able to see the White House of the confederacy, and the lovely tree covered hill campus of the university there. I returned to Alexandria, and so left the southern part of Virginia, having seen something of that which evokes such warmth when it is called 'The Old South'. I arrived back in Washington at midnight, after a railway journey demonstrating the glories of competition and private ownership; it being one hour and twenty minutes late on a two-and-a-quarter hour journey; no fog either.

I rose early again on Saturday to go into Washington, and saw successively; the National Archives; the National Gallery of Art; the Capitol; the Library of Congress; and the Supreme Court. In the National Archives are housed the records of the US and an interesting exhibition on the centennial exhibition of the Department of the Interior, showing how it has developed during its 100 years. In the Capitol, the dome of which is smaller than that of Saint Paul's, we saw the Senate and House of Representatives chamber, the President's room, and the circular staircase up which the British climbed to set fire to the building in 1814 ("here the British come," said an American as the group trooped up the stone stairs).

In the Library of Congress can be seen the original Declaration of Independence, the constitution, suitably enshrined, and a copy of the Magna Carta. The circular reading room is like that of the British Museum. In the afternoon I walked to the other end of the official 'Whitehall' area of Washington, past the fine new buildings of the Federal Reserve and the Pan American union, both surrounded by lawns, fountains and azaleas, past too the tottering White House, the shoring of its famous east end visible through the uncurtained windows.

Sunday was a beautiful day, and I attended Washington Cathedral, where there were thousands of people waiting to get in. The music at the service was splendid, accompanied by drums and trumpets as well as the organ. All the ladies were wearing the new Easter bonnets to take part in that walking of the streets which is called the 'Easter Parade', when ladies and gentlemen show off their new finery. Following that, we left for a Mexican dinner, went to a children's service at a church where Bill Glenn assists, and then went to view the Lincoln museum, housed in the Ford theatre in which he was assassinated. At this the story of Lincoln is graphically told.

We then went to a piano concert by Leonid Hambro in the Palm Court of the National Gallery of Art. This was built during 1937 to 1940 and funded by a $15,000,000 gift of a rich man called Andrew W Mellon, who was Calvin Coolidge's secretary of the Treasury. It is built of rose-white marble, and has a magnificent rotunda of dark green marble, with a statue and fountain in the centre. The music was beautiful, and we finished the day by having salmon at O'Donnell's, one of Washington's famous restaurants.

On Monday morning, we visited a modern church where the altar occupies a central position. It had no windows, and elaborate lighting effects are used instead. Unfortunately, I went to no church service there, but it was an interesting building. No less remarkable is the famous Pentagon building, in which is easy to get lost, and there is the story of the famous messenger who found it so enthralling that he came out a full colonel! The Pentagon houses the Defence Department and is five-sided, five-storied, and has five concentric connected rings of building before the inner court is reached. It is worthy of a mayor and council of its very own.

I then left Washington to travel to Carlisle near Harrisburg, the capital of Pennsylvania. Carlisle was the seat of fighting in the revolution and in the civil war, which was euphemistically called the war between the States and the South. There I attended a Rotary district conference, and was once again able to enjoy the warm Rotary welcome by the district governor and by the chairman of the foundation fellowships committee. In the evening there was a dance; refreshments at dances here are not elaborate as in England, but usually a good fruit punch is served.

In the morning there was a Rotary President's breakfast at 8 a.m., followed by a plenary session, at which I spoke, giving an informal repeat of the New York speech. I was rapturously received by all including the district governor Ernest Dunbar and past Rotary International director, and Leo Golden, the chairman of the fellowship committee. Following this there was a luncheon, and the afternoon was spent seeing a carpet factory and Carlisle barracks, some of the finest in the United States. In the evening there was a huge banquet, at which Senator Mundt of South Dakota gave an impassioned speech on communion and peace, which raised some enthusiasm in his audience. So ended an exceptionally fine conference which I was glad to be able to attend.

The train took me back to New York the following day, through the lovely rolling country of farms and hills, through Philadelphia, and the first sight of the Empire State Building seemed to announce that I was home again.

Next Monday, I go to speak at Atlantic City. Mr Zatteau is most enthusiastic about my Rotary International report and has okay'd the California trip, so full steam ahead. I have quite put the UN work from my mind, and as it has not worried me at all, I am sure it was the right decision.

I have received the sad news that Miss Cornelia Kinkead has died very suddenly. She was a cousin of the Kinkeads I stay with and she lived across the road from them. She was such a charming person of about 75.

42. ATLANTIC CITY

500 RIVERSIDE DRIVE
NEW YORK 27, N.Y.

26th April 1949

I have made three purchases this week. Both my pairs of grey trousers had seen better days, and have had to be put to one side, so I replenished with a pair of lightweight beige gabardine ones; $10 in a sale at Macy's. They fit well; all American trousers are sold with long legs and then the turnups are put on to suit the height of the purchaser, which is good for me. They are on six-day delivery, so I get them on Saturday. Then, as my father really needs his dressing gown back, I bought a seersucker bathrobe today, $5 in green, decorated with little squares of yellow and white which is very effective, and useful as I often sit in such a thing in my bedroom, which gets fuller and fuller with people!

As I have accumulated so much, I knew I should need another suitcase, and got a good one in a sale for $10. It is beige outside, with narrow bands of stripes grouped together in two wide sections and is leather bound and the rest is some sort of shiny fabric. It has a good lock and handle. The interior is red, and it has lots of pockets all over the place. It will be good for going to California, and I have such a lot to bring back to England.

The past few days have been eventful. On Saturday night, we went to an Italian restaurant and had a good meal there, and then came back to the House to see *Blithe Spirit* which was very well performed. Beryl Prendergast played the part of Elvera, and she acted the part very well, if a trifle inaudibly. The part of Madam Arcadi was changed to Baron Arcadi, to allow Roscoe Browner to get a part, but it lost effectiveness thereby.

On Sunday morning I heard Doctor Fosdick preach. I do not imagine that he has lost any of his old effectiveness, so the content was familiar. Then that afternoon I travelled with Otto Borch to the Rotary conference in Atlantic City, arriving in time for dinner. Atlantic City is a resort set in marshes with no nice country around; I would not wish to spend a holiday there. The conference was more like the ones I have heard of in Rotary district fourteen, with a running cocktail bar in the Camden Rotary club's sitting room which we made use of. I made the remark that I had best drink Scotch, as it is all exported, and is the great drink here, although I much prefer others. We had a delicious dinner, heard a boys' choir sing and then sat around talking.

On Monday morning we arose early, and following a fine breakfast of liver and bacon, we walked on the front until lunchtime as it was nice and warm. After a good luncheon, in which the Mayor of Reading gave an awfully bad speech, we ourselves spoke. I repeated the New York talk which is doing overtime these few weeks, with considerable effect, and afterwards we answered questions to the crowd's delight. Both our talks seemed to please the Rotarians and Rotary wives, many of the latter of whom came in especially to hear their little darlings.

I then returned to New York, as I wanted to be here for lectures, and to do some shopping. Here the trains still run to standard time even though we have daylight saving, so it is very confusing. The Vice-President Barkley has already missed a plane because of this.

Coming back on the train from Atlantic City, I met a most interesting and cultivated man of about 70, who was secretary of the National Academy of Sculptors. He knew all the old people in London, including the Sackvilles at Knole, and had been the London dealer of a New York firm with 'Noydeles' (phonetically) of Bond Street.

We talked of Chesterfield House, lay rectors, and I am invited to lunch with him. I was pleased to meet him as he seemed anxious to talk.

Last Friday I had Frank Mitchell here to lunch, and I introduced him to Mr de Roser, director of the International House Association, the 'old boys' organisation here. He is soon coming to England, is visiting Driscoll, and trying to find any chances of opening an International House in London. Mitchell is writing to his friend James Chuter Ede *(English Labour Politician – SMP)* about it, hoping to get something moving.

43. SOUTH PACIFIC

500 RIVERSIDE DRIVE
NEW YORK 27, N.Y.

2nd May 1949

Last Tuesday night, I went around to see Mrs Bates, one of the social staff at the House, as she has had a sudden operation for gallstones in March and is now recuperating. She has just returned to New York, having been staying in Ohio since Saturday and wanted to hear all about what I have been doing. She seems better but had a very narrow escape on the operating table.

Last Wednesday, we went to see the new musical *South Pacific*. Although it is by the same writers of *Oklahoma*, it is not a repeat, having far more 'play' in it. It is less of a continuous jollity, and in parts it is even little tragic. Its themes are about the French planter of a Pacific island (Puize, star of the Metropolitan opera), and his love for a muse of the US army, with the soldiers and sailors and their Thanksgiving Day show, and a native woman called Bloody Mary, and her expeditions into buying and selling grass skirts.

The music is lovely, and the songs are superb and haunting, with names such as *Some Enchanted Evening, Dites-moi Pourquoi, I'm as Corny as Kansas in August, Bali Hai*, and *I'm going to Wash that Man right out of my Hair*. Mary Martin, the nurse, takes her shower and lathers her hair while singing this. It will doubtless run for years and sold $500,000 of tickets before it opened.

Luckily, we managed to get early tickets, otherwise I should have had to wait until after I had left New York before seeing it! We had dinner at the Sea Fare afterwards which was delicious as usual.

On Thursday, Governor Miller of 177 Rotary International was in town, and we had lunch with him at the New York Hotel. In the afternoon, I spent a long time getting plane and train reservations for my forthcoming trip to Williamsport, and also read a good British war novel, *From the City, From the Plough*, by Alexander Baron.

On Friday, I did some laundry in the morning, and was forced to nearly steam myself to pieces, before retiring because of aches from the spring festival rehearsals. This great event took place on Saturday. From 8:30 till midnight there was alternately national displays of folk dancing and general folk dancing for everybody, followed by midnight supper and then by general folk dancing until 2:00 a.m.

We British, which included Canada, Australia, and New Zealand, did four things. First, Ann Lewis and I did the Lambeth Walk and extracted all the humour that we could from it. It was quite hilarious. I was dressed in her brown and white check slack suit and showed tartan socks. She was looking seductive in a black dress, and a silver laine wrap, lightly draped around her arms, clasped by a rose. She wore a large black veiled hat similarly rosed and had big false eyelashes. Then the Canadians did a Red Indian dance and we followed that by two girls doing the Scottish sword-dance, and then eight of us did the eightsome reel. Of course, I donned a kilt for this, and I found I could swing the kilt very well in the dance although it was extremely exhausting.

Altogether, ours was one of the best shows and we received many compliments upon it. We ended up by doing a vigorous hokey-cokey and got all the crowd joining in as well which was quite a sight it is not danced over here. Two people, who are not free with their praise, said I was "a riot and sensational," in it, and I certainly entered into the spirit of it all. Everyone was nearly dead after Scottishes, Mexican waltzes, polkas, rasbas and so on. It was one of the best evenings I have ever had. The kilt's the thing for me to wear to make a quick and favourable impression.

I am very fond of folk dancing and I have a book of folk dances to spread their fame with. Michael Herman who runs folk dancing things here is one of the top people in that field in the US. I think in England we miss a lot of fun by concentrating on modern ballroom dancing and I think folk, square and old-time dancing is the best for young people, as it is a social activity. It is also particularly good exercise.

With a great effort on Sunday, I managed to walk to the Diehl's, and go to church. We had an excellent lunch afterwards, including once again this marvellous dessert called Zabioque. They were charming as usual, and one interesting thing I found out was that he built the bridges leading to Niagara Falls from Buffalo.

Then that night I journeyed by sleeper train to Williamsport. I enjoyed the sleeper which was extremely comfortable, and I slept soundly. I was to speak at their Rotary lunch and before this in the morning I went for a nice drive through the countryside, which has beautiful apple blossom and other good English features. At the lunch there were 25 schoolboy junior Rotarians being inducted, so I addressed myself in part to them and I spoke for 30 minutes, without referring to my notes. My speech was being broadcast on the local radio station WRAK. They seemed pleased to have me and gave me $30 plus $30 travelling expenses - fancy £15 for 30 minutes of me!

I then toured the County court and County gaol. At the court I met two judges and the sheriff, all political appointments. The County Sheriff was straight out of the feature movies; fat, shirt-sleeved, hearty, and very jovial. I shall make use of him in future talks, bless him. I then flew back to New York which was a peaceful trip above the clouds. But as we had to circle several times before landing, the unpleasant ears sensation took some time to wear off.

We are not going to the Kinkead's yet awhile, they are both very tired indeed. Cornelia Kinkead's death seems to have affected them a lot, and they say they both want to sleep 24 hours a day. I think they were doing too much. Jennie has apparently been quite sick, so David and I are therefore postponing our visit.

44. DINNER WITH THE ROCKEFELLERS

500 RIVERSIDE DRIVE
NEW YORK 27, N.Y.

10th May 1949

This past week has certainly been eventful. Thursday was the first big day, when the student council trustee dinner took place. A cloud was put over things as Mr Mott had a heart attack on Tuesday, and is now resting in hospital for several weeks. After having worked at everything and taking such pride in all that was to happen, it seems to have been a cruel blow of fate.

Thanks to his preparations, everything went off very well. We first had sherry in the library with the trustees' wives. I spoke mainly with Mrs Cleveland Dodge, and she is certainly charming. Then following that, we went upstairs to the dinner, which consisted of shrimp cocktail, soup, delicious steak, and strawberry sundae. At this we rotated, each sitting at three different tables, thus meeting three different sets of people.

For the first course, I sat opposite Mr John D. Rockefeller Jnr. (now 80) and General Marshall. Marshall is a very bright conversationalist, he talked about flying and politics and looks as fit as a fiddle. Rockefeller is amiable and unpretentious. To think of the wealth he has controlled is quite amazing. He is short, stocky, with a pink pleasantly smiling face, white hair, steel rimmed glasses and a black suit.

We talked about heating houses in England. He told of freezing in Sir William Beveridge's home, and said he would always use a warming pan.

The next person I sat next to was Mrs David Rockefeller, who is vivacious. Her husband went to the London School of Economics. She talked about Williamsburg quite extensively, and how the Rockefellers personally got the furniture and other antiques from England for the houses there. She was in a blue and white ankle length dress, arranged in bands of various sized spots. She wore pearls, clasped by a sapphire, a sapphire bracelet, and a large single stone diamond engagement ring. At that time, I was also sitting opposite General Osborne.

At the third rotation, I sat opposite Mrs John D Rockefeller III, another very likeable lady. Their husbands too are tremendous people, they are the model rich family, there is no doubt. It does seem remarkable to have met such people and I shall always be able to remember it.

After the dinner, we all went into the auditorium, where we had a short musical programme. Mr Rockefeller did not speak, but he took a bow, and General Osborne told the story of how the House was founded, and how Mr Rockefeller insisted on making his gift three times as large as they requested, so that it should be self-supporting. General Marshall spoke briefly, and very well indeed, on the necessity for confidence in international understanding. After that we returned to the House room, and I fetched Mr Rockefeller's hat and very silky coat and escorted him from the House. It was indeed a wonderful evening.

On Friday, I was at Asbury Park at a Rotary district conference, where I spoke and was well received, and where I met Porter W Carswell, chairman of the New York convention committee. He was most interesting, though conservative, not to say reactionary.

I returned to the House on Saturday morning and that afternoon I went with Bill Clancy to see *Medea* by Eudipedes at the city centre with Judith Anderson, which is one of the outstanding performances of the year. It is, of course horrible, but with good acting. That evening, after a Chinese meal we celebrated Bob Andress's and Curtis Greens' birthdays.

The following day, we had a student council meeting in the morning, after which I went to Holy Communion at 12:30. I then went to purchase an azalea as a gift from the council for Mr Mott and had lunch with John Graham at Columbia University. In the afternoon we sunbathed on the roof successfully.

That evening was the candle ceremony with Mrs Roosevelt. We all met her and were introduced to her, and she was delightful. She had on a dark grey, V-neck dress, a black hat and red feather and red shoes, no makeup, and six rings, four on her left and two on her right hand. She spoke to us about the charter of human rights and our responsibilities in the world at large. I am convinced that she is a very great woman indeed.

Following her speech was the candle ceremony; the lights were dimmed to almost complete darkness, and from a large lighted candle the president of the student council lit another candle, then lit those of the student council members lighting one from the other. Then they go out to the tables and pass on the light and it is thus that from just the original large candle the auditorium changes to a blaze of light which was most effective.

Then we sang a hymn of brotherhood to the joy theme of Beethoven's *Choral Symphony*, followed by *Auld Lang Syne*, after which, holding candles, we led the way from the hall in procession. We talked a little more with Mrs Roosevelt and then saw her off after a delightful evening.

Monday was notable for seeing *Death of a Salesman* in the evening. This is a new American tragic play, probably the best written. In it every human tragedy is explored, casting unmitigated gloom over a whimpering theatre. It is a marvellous theatrical performance, but it is quite depressing as every conceivable aspect of misery is explored; economic, business, personal and moral. It is so hard to say which is the worst! Nevertheless, it is all true to life and is undoubtedly a great drama, not entertainment so much as a magnificent achievement.

Today, I have been to Governor Miller's conference at Buck Hill Falls. I travelled overnight, spoke at the meeting, and then returned by train through glorious countryside. Tom Beuson of Rotary International was sitting next to me at lunch and I liked him very much. He seems a good sort and most intelligent.

My other news is that I am now going to go to California with a group from the House in one of the girl's cars. We shall share expenses and insurance is covered. We will depart on May 29th and take eight or nine days to get there. It is a great opportunity and just what I hoped for. We shall travel via Philadelphia; Pittsburgh; Lexington in Kentucky; Saint Louis; Kansas City; Denver; Salt Lake City; Reno; and San Francisco. We shall unfortunately miss Chicago, but Dick Vermo, who is treasurer of Rotary International, was at Buck Falls today and told me, "don't give it a second thought, to go by car is so good." I shall be Rotarying at the other end, further plans later.

45. CALIFORNIA DREAMING

500 RIVERSIDE DRIVE
NEW YORK 27, N.Y.

17th May 1949

It seems hard to believe that I shall only be in New York for another ten days or so, and that this marvellous year is thus drawing towards its close. What an experience to have had, and the only thing is that I am not sure whether one should have quite such a time at such a tender age. I'm already having to remember that it will not last forever.

There has been a big change in my plans. I am not now going to California by car. You remember that the Rotarian I met on the boat getting to 'these United States', a Mr Ewart, said that if I were to speak to clubs in California, he thought they might help me with my expenses. I had a letter in February asking me when I could go, and what sort of things I wanted to see crossing the country.

Then last week I had a telegram saying that arrangements were made for me to leave from New York on May 26th, followed on Monday by a letter telling me that they had booked the route and were going to pay all my expenses! They have booked and paid for a whole tour for me, and I shall speak to maybe a dozen clubs. It is so incredibly marvellous and gracious that I jump with my well-known glee every time I think of it.

I told Mr Ewert of course that I would accept, and he has arranged it all, I have just to pick up the tickets. It so marvellous I can hardly believe it.

I leave on May 27th. My first stop will be in New Orleans, where I arrive on Saturday evening and stay until Monday morning. From there I go to the Grand Canyon, Arizona, arriving there on Wednesday morning and staying until Thursday evening, and arriving at Bakersfield in California on Friday evening. I stay in that general district for a week; then I will continue on the 10th June to Los Angeles, and the following Friday to Santa Barbara (where the Kinkeads had a weekend home), then up to San Francisco the following Tuesday.

Leaving there on June 24th, I go to Salt Lake City to stay with Bob's aunt for three days, to Chicago for a night, and I will return to New York on July 1st. Then I will probably have a weekend with the Kinkeads in Poughkeepsie, and so will be sailing home on the 7th of July. In the framework of this marvellous programme, I should be able to see most of California, and visit all the House members and Bob's friends who live there.

I shall pack most of my things up before leaving International House, and will therefore not have too much to do when I return for the last few days before sailing. I shall just keep one suitcase with me, and leave the little weekend case empty to put oddments in. I must see Cunard this week about various luggage and financial matters. Having saved $300 as my Californian expenses will be paid, I now have a good deal of money, and I shall buy a light suit for the heat and a sports shirt or two, a pair of shoes, and a pair of bathing trunks, to end all bathing trunks!

I have been to hear Visser 't Hooft speak, a Dutch Theologian who is President of the World Council of Churches. Then on Sunday morning I heard Van Dusen at Union Theological, who preached an excellent sermon in every respect on pilgrimage and faith.

On Sunday evening Burl Ives, a singer of American folk songs was here, and I bought a book of his music. Today I had an economic history exam which was not too bad, and I have a visit to a Hungarian restaurant planned tonight.

46. A SAD DEPARTURE

500 RIVERSIDE DRIVE
NEW YORK 27, N.Y.

Thursday 26th May 1949

I've bought a lot of light clothes last week for the California adventure; a lightweight oatmeal coloured suit for $30; four seersucker sports shirts striped in white and red, blue, brown and a red check which are quite gay, and I can easily wash them on my way. I also bought a natty pair of bathing trunks which are blue and red with a green and white pattern, a pair of shoes, with crepe soles which the doctor said would be all right and some little pants. I also purchased a pair of sunglasses, which I will need for California I am sure.

On Friday, I had a delightful evening at Mrs Bates' home. She is now back at work. On Saturday I worked all day, then on Sunday I went to a party at Thea Petscheli's. Her parents were amongst the wealthiest families in Czechoslovakia. They have a magnificent house, with five reception rooms, a lovely garden and two parlours and maids. We had a delightful time and sang some Gilbert and Sullivan. There was folk dancing and marvellous food.

On Monday, I worked all day, and then on Tuesday David and I travelled up to Poughkeepsie to visit the Kinkeads. They were both tired, in fact Jennie was in bed. They do too much, and to top it all their gardener has had a stroke, so we did not stay long.

We returned to New York for dinner downtown with six people from the House.

On Wednesday, I went to a beach and got quite sunburnt all over (small area excepted) then in the evening I was so tired that I just lazed around.

Today being Thursday, I did laundry this morning and went downtown this afternoon to see about the railway tickets. I went to see Mr Mott and had lunch at Champlain followed by dinner back here at International House.

I am now preparing with Bill Clancy and Bob a farewell party of great proportion including the provision of potent drinks and fruit and cheese. We are having about thirty people, so it should be good.

Packing is still to be done.

This year has been just so marvellous that it will be dreadful to leave International House tomorrow, but I shall have to steel myself even if it is to go to California.

We embark on the night of July 6th, and Cunard have been helpful with advice and details.

47. COWBOY AND WESTERN

GRAND CANYON NATIONAL PARK ARIZONA

EL TOVAR
GRAND CANYON
NATIONAL PARK
ARIZONA

Thursday June 2nd 1949

(The reader should note that this chapter contains expressions which are reflective of the era in which they were written and are now considered offensive – SMP)

I am taking up my pen to tell you how I am getting on the 3000-mile trip, to Bakersfield, California. I had hoped to write on the train to New Orleans, but that was not to be, as we had a very bumpy track, and scribble is not much use.

After a hectic few last days, I arranged to leave New York and International House and all its nice people last Friday. On Wednesday we had a picnic on Riis Beach in Long Island, and then on Thursday we had a large party in Bill Clancy's room which he, Bob and I gave.

It was quite riotous, as it was founded on seabreezes, a one-third gin, two-thirds fruit juice, which you should drink in small quantities! We had much good food as well, and most of the House heard about it. That left me with only Friday to pack; and I was ready to leave for New Orleans at 2:50 p.m. It was awfully hard to say goodbye to everyone and everything at International House, but it is done, although I shall be back there for a few days in the beginning of July.

On the train to New Orleans, I met the Unitarian minister there, and talked with him quite a good deal. The first part of the journey I had covered before on previous trips, but when I woke up on Saturday morning to find myself in the Smoky and Blue Ridge Mountains it was new to me. The first big town we hit was Atlanta, Georgia. We then travelled right on through Alabama and Mississippi, through part of the South until New Orleans. The chief thing which struck me there is the poverty and the squalor of the negroes who live in little villages all along the line which were full of Saturday afternoon crowds all watching the big train pass through.

The fields contained cotton growing, though much of the land is entirely desolate. There are some cotton mills being built there now; if they are owned by northerners the wealth goes north instead of staying to improve conditions in the South. This part of the South, from Georgia to West Texas, is very flat, with few farms, and it is much the same scenery all the way, crops alternating with flat, derelict, and undeveloped plains.

It was dark when we arrived in New Orleans at 8:40 on Saturday evening. I immediately took a taxi to the Saint Charles hotel, the chief French Hotel of the town and an incredibly good place for Rotary to have arranged for me. The town of New Orleans was originally French, and my hotel is in the Old French Quarter, where there are countless period houses with delightful iron balconies, beautiful courtyards filled with tropical and semi tropical plants, and the cathedral in Jackson Square. I had a lovely evening stroll along the streets around the hotel.

The French Quarter is of course famous for its food, and with an International House person whom I casually met that evening, I went to one of the best eateries, the Court of the Two Sisters.

In the restaurant's courtyard, surrounded by tropical plants and lighted candles, and overlooked by lovely balconies, we had mint juleps, which is the traditional drink of the Old South, and Crepes Suzettes, which are pancakes fried in brandy liqueur. They were delicious, if rich.

On Sunday morning, I went to the Roman Catholic Cathedral of Saint Louis, and then on to the Episcopalian one.

I met up with a Professor and Mrs Hathaway, who have a daughter called Maria at International House. After an excellent lunch they took me to the Huey P. Long bridge over the Mississippi, which is named after a corrupt and fascist governor of Louisiana in the thirties who ended up being assassinated.

We then went to see the garden section where the aristocracy lived 100 years ago in the times of the great wealth of New Orleans. There are huge white columned houses in the luxuriant gardens of both tropical and temperate plants. Then after that we went and looked a little more at the French Quarter and called to see General Beauregard's House. The famous author Frances Parkinson Keyes lives there, and she showed us around. She has refurbished the whole house as it was in its glory. It is a wonderful place, with a courtyard at the back and a lovely selection of furniture. In the evening we went to dinner at Galatories, one of the famous restaurants, and had a wonderful shrimp concoction and ice cream with orange liqueur.

On Monday morning, I reboarded the train and left New Orleans for the Grand Canyon. The journey passed first through the rice, sugar, tobacco and cotton fields of Louisiana, and the oilfields around Baton Rouge. Everything was absolutely flat, and as we entered East Texas the view was just of woods and swamps, nothing else. We passed through Houston, the great oil town, where there are oceans of millionaires, and where one man has just produced $18 million, and built a new hotel of already fabulous reputation.

The following morning, I woke up and looked out of the train to see 'Cowboy and Western' country just like a movie. The train then travelled for the whole day across the plains and plateaux for one thousand miles deep into the heart of Texas. Rising above that for a half day there is perfectly flat and cultivated land, just mile after mile after mile.

Then we entered the great plains of New Mexico, just grassland, not even a horse to be seen, let alone a house. During the afternoon we passed the Manzanos mountain range, and so the plains and ranches roll on and on, with here and there Indian reservations and then a great petrified forest, which is very extraordinary. This part was originally settled by the Spanish and is just so huge and bare. To think people pushed covered waggons across it is amazing!

And so yesterday morning, we finally arrived at the Grand Canyon, and I am staying at this pleasant hotel, the El Tovar. The landscape is indeed phenomenal, a huge canyon in the middle of the high plateau which has inspired the remark, "golly, what a gully!" The pictures give some idea of it, but it is so vast as to be unbelievable.

I arrived at 7 a.m. and by 9 a.m. was firmly seated on a mule, and stayed there for the sixteen-mile trip down the Canyon and back up again, with short breaks until 5 p.m. It is really quite a tiring and wearing journey as you are going down and up very steeply. You go with eight others and a cowboy guide and see it right down the mile of its great depth. It has wonderful colours, and varieties of types of scenery, reds and yellows, browns, and greens. For the first time in my life, I wore a straw hat to keep the sun off, as it is extremely hot at the bottom, where the Colorado River rushes by.

After the Canyon adventure I did not feel very energetic! Fortunately, the ranch-like hotel had lots of things to look at in the way of Indian goods of one sort or another.

I leave here tonight, and go straight to Bakersfield in California, and shall then be there for three weeks seeing goodness knows what. There seems to be everything under the sun to see there, and I expect I shall be busy as usual.

John Prior (at rear) in the Grand Canyon.
Photo: Kolb Bros Studio, Arizona.

48. CALIFORNIA LIVING

9 June 1949

After leaving the Grand Canyon, I arrived in Bakersfield, California, last Friday morning, and I have had a marvellous time in the heat ever since. I am staying at the Hotel El Tejon, which will become my Bakersfield headquarters, giving me considerable freedom. I had dinner with my sponsoring Rotarian, Mr Ewert, and his family who are extraordinarily nice, and who have arranged everything.

The weather is around 90 degrees here, but dry, so I sat in a cool courtyard reading for some time on Saturday, which was a free day for me. In the evening, I went to the graduation exercises for the junior college with Mr Ewert.

Mr and Mrs Van Ewert's house in Bakersfield. Photo: John Prior

On Sunday, I travelled to Los Angeles to meet Tyrus Harmsen, a great friend of Bob's. After lunch in Pasadena, he took me to see the Huntingdon Home art gallery, library, and grounds. Huntingdon was a railway magnate, and this was his former home. Tyrus then took me to Laguna, which is a swish resort, sixty miles to the south. We had an excellent dinner there and returned to Los Angeles in time for me to catch the late bus back to Bakersfield.

On Monday, I spent the day seeing the huge farming operation of the Kern County Hand Company, around 450,000 acres of ranch and arable land which was most interesting and instructive. It is a big business and organised as such.

The next day, I went up to Dunbar with Mr Ewert to give the first Rotary talk. I spoke on Great Britain's economic problems and it went quite well. Afterwards we drove through the great Redwood forest of Kings Canyon and the Sequoia National Park, returning to Bakersfield at 11:30 p.m.

On Wednesday, I presented my second Rotary talk at Visalia. I spent the rest of the day with Bob's brother Jerry, who is younger than Bob and married. His Mother-in-law has a swimming pool, so it was marvellous! He showed me the Wallace home in Exeter, ten miles from Visalia. Then today I spoke to the Bakersfield Rotary club at noon, had a lazy afternoon, and dined with the Ewerts tonight.

Tomorrow, we are off to Santa Barbara, after speaking at the Rotary there I shall have a free weekend for bathing and lazing on the beach. California really is something in terms of living and life!

Mr and Mrs Ewert at Sequoia National Park. Photo: John Prior

49. SANTA BARBARA

19th June 1949

I am still having a marvellous, unforgettable time. Last Friday, I went with Mr and Mrs Ewert and their family to Santa Barbara, a coast resort due west of Bakersfield, and one of the old Spanish missions to California. We stayed at a motel, which is a place where you just park your car outside and have a room. This type of accommodation is increasingly becoming the fashion in the United States. It was right on the sea front.

Santa Barbara is a centre for wealthy retired people, rather like Torquay or Bognor Regis in England. It is set in a saucer of hills and mountains, and all kinds of flowers flourish in gardens. The houses are delightful, and the shops, many with a simulated Spanish flavour, are pleasant. The mission itself with church and living quarters is likewise beautiful, mainly because of the pinkish coloured stone used, which looks splendid against a blue sky. Unfortunately, the weather while we were there was rather cold and misty, so I could not sea bathe as much as I would have liked. We stayed there over Saturday and Sunday and returned Sunday night.

The Kinkeads, who had a House there for winters, had given me some addresses, but apart from phoning greetings I did not visit them, as I thought I would more enjoy just wandering around and sampling some of the good places to eat. For lunch on Saturday, I had a Mexican meal at the El Peseo, and in the evening I went to The Talk of the Town which served as good a meal as I have had here in America, and it had delightful atmosphere with subdued lights and excellent service. I had; a shrimp cocktail; French onion soup; mixed salad; sweetbreads *financière*; hollandaise asparagus; and baked Idaho potatoes, all dressed up with the most delicious sauces and very tasty, followed a special wine-covered sundae.

The Bakersfield–Californian newspaper had the following report after our visit to Santa Barbara:

"*Mr and Mrs War Van Velsen Ewert, accompanied by their family and Mr John Prior of Croydon, England, sojourned in Santa Barbara over the weekend. Mr Prior said that while the Ewert family found the sea too cold for their liking, the rigours of the English climate had well prepared him for the ocean*".

I do remember saying I had not thought the ocean as cold as the Ewerts did, but to whom I cannot think and how it got in the newspaper, the writer alone knows!

On Sunday, the president of the student body of the University of California in Santa Barbara invited me to spend the afternoon with him. He is an honorary member of the Santa Barbara Rotary club, where I had met him on Friday. He married an Australian girl after having sailed the Pacific alone in a boat to join the RAAF before the USA joined the war and is having a book published on the subject in October, which I shall try to read. He took me to a garden wedding of one of his friends from college, and then on to a baccalaureate graduation service. The garden wedding was very pretty on grassy slopes, amid lupins, high over Santa Barbara and in the Riviera section of the town.

Then I was back at Bakersfield for four days, on three of which I successfully spoke to various Rotary clubs. On the first day, Monday, I spoke at the Shafter club, and then returned to the hotel spending the rest of the day alone including seeing a film in the evening called *The Stratton Story*.

On Tuesday I spoke at the Oakdale club, and then in the afternoon Bob's friend, Clifton Wignell, from San Francisco, came and stayed at the hotel until Thursday, that being the only way that we could meet. He was most interesting, and we shall correspond. It is extremely hot all the time here in Bakersfield, 90 to 110 degrees.

In the afternoon, we were invited for cocktails to a Mr Thrasher's lovely home, he is another Rotarian. His son, daughter and son-in-law were there, and I duly entertained them with full accounts of my life in America. They thought it a great show. The evening, Clifton Wignell and I spent together at the hotel, then on Wednesday, I travelled to speak at the Taft Rotary. Taft is at the end of beyond, deep in the desert and surrounded by oil fields. That evening we went to Mr Ewert's after dinner for talk and ice cream and stayed until 11 p.m.

The next day after seeing Clifton Wignell off at the station, I attended a Rotary lunch. A Rotary fellow from New Zealand was there, he gave a rather more intellectual and earnest talk than my party piece! Mr Ewert assured me afterwards that he thought my type of speech more suited to the occasion as I usually find something funny to say.

Clifton Wignell outside Hotel El Tejon, Bakersfield CA. Photo: John Prior

That night, a rich automobile dealer invited me out. He has another beautiful home, and assisted by a couple of scotches, I gave a resume of my more hilarious US experiences for him and his family. We then went out to a good steak dinner, and they generously gave me a posh crocodile leather key case in modern design. After dinner we listened to their *South Pacific* records.

Then on Friday, I went to Los Angeles to a lunch with the British consul general. He is very likeable, and we shall meet again on the Queen Mary. His opinion is that Bevan has more loyalty from all and sundry in the foreign office than any of his predecessors did, and they think he is marvellous.

In the evening, I went to a dinner and meeting of new Rotarians and I spoke as part of the Rotary information service to them.

I stayed that night with Mr Ralph Cardozo, a Rotarian who has made a small fortune in greetings cards and lives amongst the film stars in Beverly Hills. He has a lovely Mediterranean-type house, with a courtyard and a terraced garden offering a view over the Los Angeles sprawl, which is pretty at night. Both the rich and not-so-rich in California often have loggias to entertain their guests. Californian flowers and gardens have something of the luxuriance of the English ones which those in other parts of the US often do not.

On Saturday morning, I went for a tour around Warner Brothers Studio with a Mr Louis Fisher. I was lucky enough to see both Humphrey Bogart and James Cagney at work which was interesting to say the least of it. The film industry is an extraordinary business. Mr Fisher and his family entertained me for the weekend. Then following that, I went for a drive around Los Angeles and its area, and to a party for foreign students in the evening. On Sunday, I went in the morning for an air trip around Southern California in a small plane. I am now off to Fresno and shall then be in San Francisco tonight.

50. THE TOP OF THE MARK

San Francisco Overland
Chicago and North Western System
Union Pacific Railroad
Southern Pacific

Enroute 24 Jun

Friday, on the way to Salt Lake City. *(24th June 1949)*

Last Monday, there was a most amusing incident when I spoke at Fresno Rotary. Their normal programme consisted of an American Medical Association doctor speaking against the socialised medicine plan of Truman. We sat next to each other and had a polite interesting conversation. I the spoke for seventeen minutes prior to 1 p.m., and my speech did not include National Health or any related subjects. I did however include the statement that I believed before one spoke of other countries, it was well to understand their histories and to visit them.

Then the doctor got up for his talk at 1 p.m. and commenced by apologising for not fitting my requirements. He delivered a lengthy diatribe about socialised medicine; he overran his time and of course extracted what ammunition he could from Bevan. He was not too good a speaker, and then said he felt awkward attacking our health scheme, as I had just said that I thought to speak about countries one should visit them. Afterwards, despite a 99.9% agreement with him, all the Rotarians seemed to presume I should like to continue the debate by answering him and disagreeing with his arguments, and they would relish the spectacle of a lively session by my doing so.

Naturally, I was much amused, and Mr Ewert, who is sympathetic to the Labour government, said that my being there, evidently unintentionally put him off his stroke. The Rotarian is a strange breed. I think this is one of the richer incidents of my American Story.

I spent the afternoon in the lovely home of a Rotarian who is an architect, catching the train for San Francisco at 5:45 p.m. and arriving at the Hotel Stewart on Monday night at 10:15 p.m.

San Francisco is the most fascinating and beautiful city, and to approach it across the bridge from Oakland is truly wonderful in every way. Although it is often encased in light fog, when I arrived it was a bright starlit night, and the whole place looked wondrous, brilliant, and enchanting. From Oakland across the Bay Bridge, the city is a mass of twinkling light, with the Golden Gate Bridge, hovering, almost mystically, to the right. The hotel here was good and very central and, even though it was 11 p.m. I immediately went to the Top of the Mark. This is a wonderful cocktail lounge, on the 20th Storey of the Mark Hopkins hotel, on top of Nob Hill, the highest hill in San Francisco, and the view from here was wondrous. From it the whole panorama of city, bay, ocean, and bridges is unfolded, with soft blue lights in ceaseless array. The whole of the city is very varied. The cable cars of antique design go up near-vertical terraced hills to exquisite places like the Mark Hopkins and are very adventurous to ride.

Then on Tuesday, I went to the San Francisco Rotary and then met Margaret Lipman from International House. She took me on a one of the very traditional cable cars. It was quite exciting as the streets are very steep hills arranged in step like fashions. We went to Chinatown, and to Gumps, which is a luxury store. We returned to her place in Oakland for dinner. Her father is owner of San Francisco's emporium, like Peter Jones in London, and therefore rich, and they have a swimming pool, which we used. The rest of the evening we talked.

On Wednesday, I delivered my very last US speech to the Berkeley Rotary club, and visited the huge and fine University of California there. I also went to the Berkeley International House, which is built in a Moorish style, and then went to see an aunt of Bob's.

Yesterday, I visited the delightful Stanford University at Palo Alto, which was Bob's university. The Lipmans then met me and we had lunch at a good restaurant, at no cost to me. We visited Golden Gate Park and after that went to Blum's which is a candy store of great wonder.

I embarked the train today, having bought a marvellous book on San Francisco; I think it will be one of my ever-prized possessions. The train has just stopped at Sacramento, and then continues to New York via Salt Lake City.

51. AN EMOTIONAL FAREWELL

500 RIVERSIDE DRIVE
NEW YORK 27, N.Y.

July the 5th 1949

This is my last night in New York. It seems impossible that my year here is over, and I cannot settle to write much down.

The Salt Lake and Chicago parts of my trip went well. Upon returning here, I said goodbye to the Diehls at church, and had a brief visit to the Kinkeads last weekend. I went to the theatre on Saturday night and then I sent my luggage to the boat today. It is quite a large liner and we embark between 8 p.m. and 12 midnight tomorrow.

It will be wonderful to be home again, even though the feelings will be very mixed indeed. Right now, I am too muddled mentally, and I guess emotionally, to think clearly. I do not really know how American I have become, but having loved the land so, and being so friendly with Americans, and having lived with one, it will be strange if I am still unadulterated English.

I do not expect to be bringing very much food with me - no dollars left!

It has been, quite frankly, an incredible year.

John Prior, Helen Carr, Unknown, on board the Queen Mary, returning from New York. Photo: John Prior.

EPILOGUE

After his return to England on the Queen Mary, John Miskin Prior subsequently entered the priesthood in the Anglican Church and went on to become a vicar of village churches in the West Country of England.

He never forgot his friends in the United States and continued to correspond with them every year. Some of his American friends, including his roommate Bob Wallace at International House, visited him in England.

In 1984 he returned to the United States for the first time since his studies there, and stayed with Bob Wallace, now Professor of Oriental Art at the University of California, and Tyrus Harmsen and Margaret Lucas, other friends from that period.

In 1996, now retired, he again visited the United States, visiting his friend from International House, Rees Outwater, at his home in Burlington, Vermont, staying again with Bob Wallace in California, and again visiting Margaret Lucas, now living in Honolulu.

He passed away in 2014, having kept the memories of his time studying in New York alive, through his correspondence.

Bob Wallace with John Prior in San Diego, California, August 1984. Photo: John Prior.

Rees Outwater (seated) with his wife and John Prior, November 1996. Photo: John Prior.

~ THE END ~

PLEASE REVIEW AN ENGLISHMAN IN NEW YORK

If you enjoyed *An Englishman in New York*, please consider leaving a review, to inform other readers of your experience.

I've made it super-easy for you. All you have to do is visit the link below or click the QR code, and it'll take you straight to the right page.

Thanks so much, it means a lot to me.

Simon

smarturl.it/englishmanreview

ALSO BY SIMON MICHAEL PRIOR:
THE COCONUT WIRELESS

When Simon and Fiona embark on a quest to track down the Queen of Tonga, they have no idea they'll end up marooned on a desert island.

No idea they'll encounter an undiscovered tribe, rescue a drowning actress, learn jungle survival from a commando, and attend cultural ceremonies few Westerners have seen.

As they find out who hooks up, who breaks up, who cracks up, and who throws up, will they fulfil Simon's ambition to see the queen, or will they be distracted by insomniac chickens, grunting wild piglets, and the easy-going Tongan lifestyle?

Read the first few chapters FREE by visiting the link, or scanning the QR code:

Smarturl.it/lookinsidecoconut

An Englishman in New York: The Memoirs of John Miskin Prior 1948-49

ALSO BY SIMON MICHAEL PRIOR: THE SCENICLAND RADIO

When English city boy Simon follows his girlfriend across the world to her family farm in remotest New Zealand, he has no idea he'll be force-fed a meal of beetle larva, get pushed off the road by half a house, and be inspected by indignant penguins and flattened by a giant leaf-blower.

As he poisons the milk, dive-bombs the bulls, and loses the herd of cows in a river, will he ever learn to be a farmer, or will he have to stop impersonating a country boy, and return to London?

Read the first few chapters FREE by visiting the link, or scanning the QR code:

Smarturl.it/lookinsidescenicland

ALSO BY SIMON MICHAEL PRIOR: THE POMEGRANATE BUSKER

When London boy Simon dreams of becoming a New Zealand rock star, he has no idea he'll duet with a suspected murderer, model for posters with a dairy cow, accidentally present the weather on the radio and be upstaged by an apple crumble.

As he struggles to impersonate Elvis, forgets the most important birthday song and scares away a hen party, will he ever realise his rock star ambitions, or will he have to pack away his guitar and abandon his dreams forever?

Find out, in The Pomegranate Busker, the third book in the South Pacific Shenanigans series.

Read the first few chapters for free by visiting this link or scanning the QR code:

smarturl.it/lookinpomegranate

PHOTOS TO ACCOMPANY AN ENGLISHMAN IN NEW YORK

The following resources are available at

simonmichaelprior.com

- Photographs of New York, Poughkeepsie and Williamsburg in 1948/9
- Photographs of The Grand Canyon and California in 1949
- International House brochure from 1948
- Morningside Heights and Columbia University brochure from 1948
- Order of Service marking the birth of Prince Charles from 1948
- Petitpas Restaurant brochure from 1949

Please head over to my website or scan the QR code and click the book's cover.

ABOUT THE AUTHOR

Simon Michael Prior insists on inflicting all aspects of life on himself so that his readers can enjoy learning about his latest trip / experience / disaster / emotional breakdown (insert phrase of your choice).

During his extended adolescence, now over forty years long, he has lived on two boats and sunk one of them; sold houses, street signs, Indian food and paper bags for a living; visited almost fifty countries and lived in three; qualified as a scuba divemaster; nearly killed himself learning to wakeboard; trained as a search and rescue skipper with the Coast Guard, and built his own house without the benefit of an instruction manual.

Simon is as amazed as anyone that the house is still standing, and he now lives in it by the sea with his wife and twin daughters, where he spends his time regurgitating his experiences on paper before he has so many more that he forgets them.

Website: **simonmichaelprior.com**
Email: **simon@simonmichaelprior.com**
Facebook: **@simonmichaelprior**
Instagram: **@simonmichaelprior**
Twitter: **@simonmichaelpri**

If you would like to receive a regular newsletter about Simon and his writing, and be the first to find out about new releases, please sign up to his mailing list here:

simonmichaelprior.com

ACKNOWLEDGEMENTS

A big thank you to Victoria Twead and all the members of the Facebook group 'We Love Memoirs', for befriending me, encouraging me, educating me, reassuring me, and driving me forward. Thank you to Beth Haslam and Annemarie Rawson for taking the time to give me your advice, guidance and for being a shoulder when I needed it. Thank you to David Gaughran, Victoria Twead, Meg LaTorre and Dave Chesson for informative courses, tips and useful tools. Thank you to Jeff Bezos, for giving independent authors a platform on which to publish our writing. And thank you so much to my father, for never throwing anything away!

WE LOVE MEMOIRS

An Englishman in New York: The Memoirs of John Miskin Prior 1948-49

www.ingramcontent.com/pod-product-compliance
Lightning Source LLC
Chambersburg PA
CBHW022055290426
44109CB00014B/1110